Historic Charlottesville Tour Book

Historic Charlottesville Tour Book

Charlottesville's Historic
Resource Task Force

—in conjunction with—

The Albemarle County
Historical Society
The McIntire Building
200 Second Street, N.E.

Charlottesville, Virginia 22902

Contributors

EDITOR - Frank E. Grizzard, Jr.

DESIGNER - Lorena Perez of Imagine Design.

CARTOGRAPHER - Jim Herndon.

PHOTOGRAPHER - Rick Britton.

PHOTOGRAPHER'S ASSISTANT - Victoria Britton.

PRINTER - Lexis Publishing.

AUTHORS - The members of the Albemarle County Historical Society Publications Committee: Coy Barefoot, Eugenia Bibb, Vesta Lee Gordon, Joy Perry, Gayle Schulman, and Co-chairmen Rick Britton and Garrett Smith.

The Albemarle County Historical Society

Membership in the Society is open to anyone interested in the history of Charlottesville and Albemarle County. The Society invites institutional as well as individual members. Contributions to the Society are tax deductible.

Inquiries regarding membership in the Albemarle County Historical Society, or about its annual Magazine or other publications, should be made to the director, the McIntire Building, 200 Second Street, N.E., Charlottesville, Va. 22902, or call (434) 296-1492.

ISBN 0-9722733-0-1

Acknowledgements

The Publications Committee would like to thank Gayle Schulman, and committee members Robert D. Cross and Ann L. Southwell for their support on this project. Special thanks to the staff at the Albemarle County Historical Society: Director Lynne Heetderks, Librarian Margaret M. O'Bryant, past and current Assistant Directors for Management Sandy DeKay and Sarah Hamseldt, and Volunteer Coordinator Sarah Lawrence. We also received much-needed help and guidance from the members of Charlottesville's Historic Resources Task Force: Co-chairmen Mark Beliles and Coy Barefoot and Jim Wootten; Rick Britton, Florence Bryant, Mary Hill Caperton, Bobbye Cochran, Helena Devereux, Jim Eddins, ex-Mayor Francis Fife, Ben Ford, Winston Churchill Gooding, Fred Heblich, Jr., Lynne Heetderks, Ingrid Smyer Kelly, and Garrett Smith, as well as Charlottesville Strategic Planner Satyendra Singh Huja.

This book would not have seen the light of day if it had not been for our many gracious proofreaders, and volunteer tour-takers: Jean Barnett, Ned Berkeley, Victoria Britton, Mary Hill Caperton, Helena Devereux, O. Allan Gianniny, Jr., Sue Howland, Arnold Jensen, Bob Kuhlthau, Lee Lewis and assistant, Margaret M. O'Bryant, Joy Perry, Peigi Rockwell, Charlotte Shelton, Ann Southwell, Sue Weber, Sally Whaley, and Jean Wooley. We give special thanks to K. Edward Lay, Cary D. Langhorne Professor of Architecture, University of Virginia.

The Publications Committee is especially grateful to this project's financial contributors: Lexis Publishing, the Charlottesville-Albemarle Convention and Visitor's Bureau, the Perry Foundation, the City of Charlottesville, the Albemarle County Historical Society, Mr. John J. Owen, and Preservation Piedmont.

For Further Information

For information about these, and other, tours—including guided tours of historic downtown—write to the Albemarle County Historical Society at 200 Second Street, NE, Charlottesville, VA 22902, call (434) 296-1492, or visit the Web-site at http://monticello.avenue.org/achs/home.html.

The University of Virginia offers tours, beginning at the Rotunda, every day at 10 and 11 a.m., and 2, 3, and 4 p.m. For more information call the University Guide Service at (434) 924-3239 or visit the Web-site at http://www.uvaguides.org.

Introduction

Charlottesville is truly a remarkable place. With its many parks, museums and art galleries—as well as countless cultural events—Charlottesville, Virginia, is synonymous for quality of life. Founded in 1762, the city is also amazingly rich in history. Forever associated with Central Virginia's most famous native son, Thomas Jefferson—whose mountaintop villa, Monticello, watches over the city from the east—Charlottesville has also been home to Edgar Allan Poe; Dr. Walter Reed, the "conqueror of yellow fever;" and Anastasia Manahan, pretender to the last Russian royal family. Daniel Boone was captured here (during the American Revolution), Meriwether Lewis (of Lewis & Clark fame) was born near here, and fifth U.S. President James Monroe practiced law here. Among the many other notables who have walked our streets are George Armstrong Custer, who fought at the Little Big Horn, well-known artist Georgia O'Keeffe, and novelist William Faulkner.

With this book we are proud to offer 10 tours, some walking and some driving, that guide visitors along these same tree-lined lanes. Chock-full of architectural detail, the tours also provide wonderful glimpses into Charlottesville's historic past. It is our sincere hope that our visitors enjoy them as much as we have enjoyed putting them together.

Please note that aside from the public parks and public buildings listed in these pages, most of the structures described are private homes. Their inclusion on our tours must not be taken as a license to trespass on private property.

The Albemarle County Historical Society Publications Committee

How To Use this Book

The numbered stops in this tour book are keyed to the numbers located on each tour's map. Locate the map pages in the table of contents. The maps are coupled between tours (i.e. between tours A and B, C and D, E and F, G and H, and I and J.) The "While you are in the Neighborhood" sections include sites that are nearby. Their stops are numbered only if their locations can be found on that tour's map.

Driving and/or walking directions between stops are printed in italics.

Albemarle County Historical Society
The McIntire Building

Historic Charlottesville Tour Book

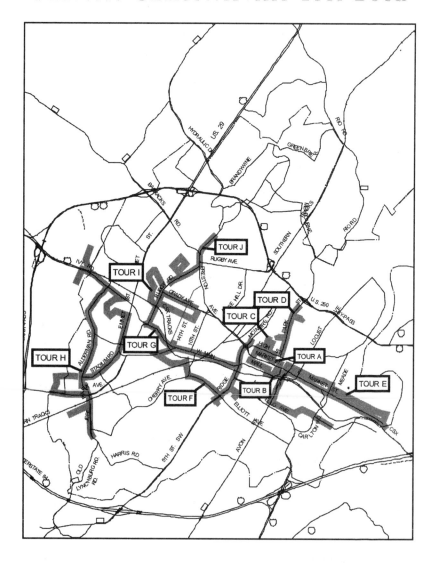

Historic Charlottesville Tour Book

Tour A

COURTHOUSE DISTRICT

Exploitation of resources, not the creation of commercial towns, drove the initial British settlement of colonial Virginia. Albemarle County, formed in 1744 with a courthouse but no town near the James River, gained enough population for the General Assembly of the colony to subdivide it in the spring of 1761. Later, a new centrally located courthouse was built atop a ridge close to the Rivanna River, and near the road connecting the great valley of Virginia to the markets of the Tidewater. The government authorized Thomas Walker, local member of the legislature, physician, explorer, surveyor, merchant, and a guardian of the youthful Thomas Jefferson to lay out and sell 56 half-acre lots for a town adjacent to the new courthouse. Charlottesville's name honors Charlotte of Mecklenburg-Strelitz, the bride of King George III. Other examples of early ties to England include the naming of the Rivanna River for Queen Anne and the James River for King James I. In the years since, the community has weathered frontier life, occupation by two different enemy forces, and has witnessed the evolution of transportation, economic challenges, and social changes.

Tours A and B describe a circuit walking tour from the Courthouse at Park Street and Jefferson and back, about 1.5 miles or about 1.5 hours. Doing the Courthouse or Downtown sections separately can shorten this tour. Take as much as your time and interest allows or stop midway for a snack or rest. They reveal evidence of both continuity and change as Charlottesville-Albemarle has evolved from a frontier neighborhood into a complex community that is as proud of its past as it is of its newly achieved modernity. To learn more, come by or call the Albemarle County Historical Society (Tour A, site 11), (434) 296-1492, or visit its web site at: http://monticello.avenue.org/achs/home.html.

A wood frame colonial courthouse was built on a two-acre public square on a ridge that continues to the north on Park Street (see Tour D) and west of the flood plain of the Rivanna River. Commerce was centered around the courthouse. Two-storied mercantile buildings housed shops downstairs and residences above. Court days occurred just once a month, so the courthouse served as a community center and place for public worship for several denominations as well as the legal and governmental center. In 1779 the town consisted of a courthouse, a tavern, and about a dozen houses. By 1835 there were about two hundred comfortable houses (most made of brick), four houses of worship, three large hotels, one tavern, two book stores, two druggists, twenty stores, and two coaches a week to Alexandria. The commercial center shifted to Main Street in the 1840s. In 1888 Charlottesville became a city independent of Albemarle County, with its own courts and taxes.

Stand near the corner of Park and Jefferson streets to view these buildings. Walk along the Park Street side of the Courthouse. Look across Park Street at four buildings; start by looking at the two-story one on the right. (Additional information is available on historical markers and in the kiosk.)

1 **300 Court Square (c.1854)** For over 150 years, buildings here have provided food and lodging for visitors. The Eagle Tavern, a wood frame structure with a porch across the front, was standing here by 1791. This brick replacement continued to serve those gathered for business and pleasure on court days. By the mid-1800s it was not unusual for the hotel to feed 200 people and care for 250 horses during monthly meetings of the court. Public dances, political parties and victory celebrations filled its spacious parlor. This building also served for two years as the headquarters of Federal occupying forces after the Civil War. The structure continued as hotel rooms into the 1960s. It is now office space.

2 **Number "Nothing" (1820s) and 6th Street Buildings (1820s-1860s)** Built as a mercantile duplex, this temple-form building with its pediment and fine proportions shows how Jefferson's design for the University of Virginia filtered into local building practice. With surrounding buildings already numbered, and no sequence possible, the building acquired the unusual address of "0" Court Square. Auctions of goods and slaves were held adjacent to this building and on the courthouse steps. In the 1820s, the brick building behind and to the right was a storehouse for merchant James Leitch. Next to it stretching down 6th Street were three frame buildings housing a privately funded village library, a whiskey dealer, and a Swiss watchmaker whom Jefferson had enticed to come to Charlottesville from Europe. The frame buildings were replaced by these brick structures beginning in the 1830s.

3 **300 Park Street (1832)** The present building, erected as a townhouse, is on the site of the Swan Tavern that briefly housed Virginia's House of Delegates in 1781. Under threat from British

forces, Governor Thomas Jefferson and Virginia's government quit Richmond on 10 May and reconvened in Charlottesville on 28 May, in effect moving the capital of Virginia here. The British, intent on capture, continued their pursuit. On the night of 3 June, Jack Jouett, son of the Swan's owner, happened to be at Cuckoo Tavern in Louisa County when he saw a British force of 250 mounted men under Colonel Banastre Tarleton headed for Charlottesville. Jouett guessed their intentions. Using horse trails and back roads he rode through the night to warn Jefferson, Patrick Henry, Richard Henry Lee, and other members of the General Assembly that included the fathers of two future American presidents, Benjamin Harrison and John Tyler. A few legislators were captured, among them the representative from what is now Kentucky, Daniel Boone, who was released a day later. Most legislators fled to safety in Staunton. Tarleton's men spared the town from destruction but destroyed some court records and military stores.

4 **Town Hall, 350 Park Street (1851) or Levy Opera House (1888)** Town Hall was built by private interests to serve as an auditorium, and during the last half of the 19th century railroads brought traveling plays, opera singers, instrumentalists, novelty acts, dancers and magicians to perform on its stage. In 1888, Jefferson Monroe Levy, owner of Monticello, remodeled the hall into a "modern" opera house seating 800. Today it houses office space.

Turn around to see the rear of the Albermarle County Courthouse, the oldest part of the structure. Then walk to the front of the building.

5 **Albemarle County Courthouse (1803, c.1859, c.1870s, 1938)** The first courthouse was a wooden building costing £375.10. Its grounds held the usual whipping post (restored as late as 1857), stocks, and pillory. It was replaced in 1803 by the rear wing of the existing brick building. As the town's only large public space, it served as a court, a polling place, and a meeting place for the University of Virginia's first Board of Visitors. Episcopalians, Presbyterians, Methodists, and Baptists took turns holding religious services here before the town's first churches were built beginning in the 1820s. After Jefferson retired to Monticello in 1809, he was a frequent visitor here, as were his friends James Madison and James Monroe. The courtroom remains in use today. The southern wing, which forms the front, was built just before the Civil War in the Gothic Revival style popular at the time, with a stucco exterior and octagonal stair towers flanking the entrance. Its columned portico was added in the 1870s, and a WPA project in the 1930s remodeled the building to conform to the classical style of the earlier section. In front of the building is the Confederate Soldier Memorial, with a bronze figure titled "At the Ready," erected in 1909. Two smoothbore, twelve-pounder Napoleon cannons like those used by both armies in the Civil War flank it.

Walk westward in front of the Courthouse to the Stonewall Jackson statue.

A walk around Jackson Park and down Jefferson Street reflects the growth of Charlottesville in the late 1800s and early 1900s into a typical southern town.

6 **Jackson Park (1918)** Sculpted by Charles Keck (1875—1951) this statue of General Thomas J. "Stonewall" Jackson on Little Sorrel (1921) has been called one of the world's finest equestrian statues, and along with the surrounding park is one of many gifts to the city from philanthropist Paul Goodloe McIntire, (1860—1952). The son of a local druggist, McIntire prospered on the New York stock exchange, and after 1918 spent much of his fortune to benefit his hometown. The McKee block, a group of pre-Civil War buildings facing the Courthouse between Jefferson an_ High streets, was razed to make room for the park and statue. Housing a grocery, dry goods store, hatter, tailor, hotel, and the print shop of the town's first newspaper, the McKee block had been the town's commercial center in the early 19th century.

Look north across High Street by walking to the far side of the park.

7 **County Jail (1875)** Look down the long driveway to view the gray stone jail with its seven cells surrounded by an 18-inch thick brick wall. It held as many as 35 prisoners. The last public hanging in Virginia took place here in 1904. The jail was in operation until 1977. It is not in use today.

8 **Juvenile and Domestic Relations Court, 411 E. High Street (1902)** To the far right is the Juvenile Court, which is housed in the former Elks Lodge building, remodeled after a fire in the 1940s.

9 **City of Charlottesville Courthouse, (1962) 315 E. High Street** To the far left is the City Courthouse with a cupola and weather vane.

Walk south past the Jackson statue with the County Courthouse on your left then westward along Jefferson Street two blocks to 2d Street, N.E. This tour intersects with Tour D at the corner of Park Street and High Street.

Places of Worship on Jefferson Street

A s you walk west on Jefferson, you will pass through what was, and still is, a center for the town's worshiping community. On the left side of the street is the site of the first building of the First Baptist Church (1831). Later it was moved one block further west on Jefferson Street. In 1977 that congregation built a new church on Park Street (see Tour D, site 17). Before it was finished the old building burned.

Further down the block on the right is Temple Beth-Israel, which was formed in 1860. When the federal government claimed the temple's first site near here on E. Market Street to build a post office and courthouse in 1904, the Temple was relocated here at 3d and Jefferson Streets. In 1995 an architecturally complimentary addition was constructed. Reflecting the bonds among Charlottesville's religious communities, the temple's addition hosted the Charlottesville Catholic school during the new school's first two years. Diagonally across the street is the site of Holy Comforter Catholic Church the town's first Roman Catholic church, erected in 1880 and replaced in 1925.

Down the street on the right is the First United Methodist Church (1924). Before moving to this building, the Methodist Church had occupied two earlier buildings on Water Street. Early national leaders of the Methodist

Church, including Francis Asbury and Thomas Coke, visited the Charlottesville area in the early 19th century. While standing on the steps of the Methodist Church look through and beyond Lee Park to the right at First Christian Church on Market Street, built in 1897 to replace its first building, dating to 1836. Alexander Campbell, founder of the Disciples of Christ, preached in the original church many times. A block to the left of the Christian Church, at the corner of 2d and Market streets, are the sites for the first two buildings of Charlottesville Presbyterian Church, before the congregation moved to the present building on Park Street in 1955 (see Tour D, site 6).

Farther down Jefferson Street is Christ Episcopal Church. The first building for Christ Episcopal Church faced Jefferson Street at the corner of 2d Street, N.W. Completed in 1826, it was the earliest church building erected in the town. It was replaced in 1896 by the present stone building that faces High Street (see Tour C, site 1).

10 **109 E. Jefferson Street (1814)** Home to John Russell Jones (1787—1860) the merchant of number "Nothing" Park Street (see Tour A, site 2). It was known as the "Social Hall" by the friends of his ten children, this house features elements typical of local building in the Federal era, including lintels with corner blocks over the windows, an arched fanlight admitting southern light to a central hall, and fine brickwork. Rigid symmetry is maintained by false window blinds on the east facade. The present porch is a later addition. General John Marshall Jones, who commanded the Stonewall Brigade, grew up in this house. He was killed at the Wilderness and is interred in Maplewood Cemetery (see Tour E, site 1).

Cross Jefferson Street to the statue of Robert E. Lee and his horse, Traveller.

The Civil War in Charlottesville

In 1861 Charlottesville men formed the Monticello Guard and the Albemarle Rifles, two of ten companies in the 19th Virginia Infantry Regiment of the Confederate Army. The 19th Virginia fought in ten major battles and many skirmishes, among them First Manassas, Williamsburg, Gettysburg, Cold Harbor, and Petersburg. By the summer of

1861, 1,600 men from Albemarle had enlisted in various regiments. Away from the war front, yet accessible by rail and road, Charlottesville functioned as a General Hospital that treated more than 21,000 soldiers during the war years. Most were sick rather than wounded. Town and University doctors, men, women, and slaves worked to restore soldiers to health. Arriving refugees and residents risked exposure to the diseases that ravaged the soldiers, which compounded health problems. In March 1865 Union General Philip Sheridan occupied the undefended town for a few days.

11 Lee Park This park with its statue was another gift from Paul Goodloe McIntire, who intended the park as a memorial to his parents. The statue of General Robert E. Lee on his horse Traveller (1924) was sculpted by Henry M. Shrady (1871—1921), and after his death was completed by Leo Lentelli (1879—1961). The millstones are said to be from Thomas Jefferson's father's farm at Shadwell. This park swiftly became a focus of the emerging city. By 1925, within one block of the park, were the original library, the post office and U.S. District Court, seven religious buildings, an "old folks" home, a hospital, and an elementary school. The Jefferson Madison Regional Library main branch is now housed in the former post office and court building on the corner of 2d, N.E., and Market Streets.

12 200 2d. Street, N.E. McIntire Library/Albemarle County Historical Society (1921) The Albemarle County Historical Society houses an outstanding geneology and local history collection. Among its other offerings open to the public are exhibits on topics of local history and a variety of guided tours. The Beaux-arts style building with Corinthian columns opened its doors in 1921 as the city's first publicly supported library. The library building, books and furnishings were also paid for by Paul Goodloe McIntire (see Tour A, site 6).

Leave Lee Park continuing westward on Jefferson Street.

13 100 W. Jefferson Street (1899) The brick building diagonally across from the Methodist Church housed the Magruder Sanitarium, now offices for Christ Episcopal Church. This was the first hospital in Charlottesville to be constructed with wide halls and a stairway for the accommodation of wheel chairs and stretchers. Two years later the University of Virginia Hospital opened and in 1904 Martha Jefferson Hospital was founded.

Cross 2d Street N.W., and turn left (south) on it..

14 **201 2d Street, N.W., McGuffey School/Art Center (1916)** Opened as the city's white elementary school, the colonial revival school building was named for William Holmes McGuffey (1800—1873), editor of the widely used McGuffey Readers. The building served as a city school until 1975, when it was converted into a center for the area's art  community. Local artists in residence have studios in the building, all of which are open to the public when the artists are at work. The Gallery is open during business hours. Numerous other private studios and art galleries are located on or near the Downtown Mall.

15 **Market Street** This street was named for the early 1800s market houses that stood in the middle of the street. Glance to your left on the corner at the concrete block building (c.1908), 113 W. Market Street, former home to the Velle family, members of the Greek community. Early 1900s catalogs from Sears Roebuck included a $63.75 easy-to-use concrete block-making machine with eight special molds and accessories. A local contractor used several molds to create decorative blocks for this home. View this building as "modern" technology providing a fireproof inexpensive home.

Cross Market Street at the light and continue south on the right side for a block.

16 **115 2d Street, N.W. (1947)** The Elks Rivanna Lodge entrance will be on your right after you cross Market Street. It was organized in 1914 by members of the African-American community.

This is the end of Tour A. To begin Tour B continue walking south, turn right on the brick Downtown Pedestrian Mall and walk toward the open area. To start Tour C retrace your steps north on 2d. Street N.W. past McGuffey school/ Art Center on your left. Go one block north to High Street.

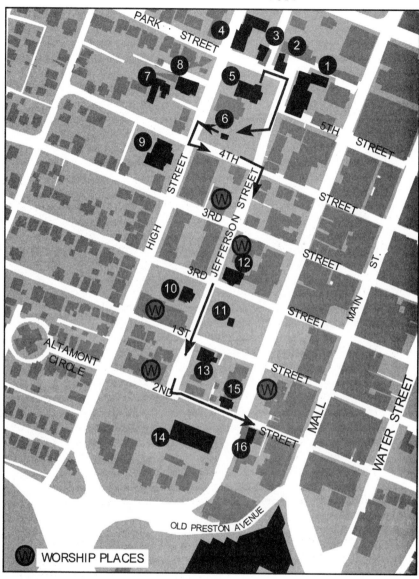

WORSHIP PLACES

Tour A

1 300 Court Square
2 Number Nothing
3 300 Park Street
4 Town Hall
5 Albemarle County Courthouse
6 Jackson Park
7 County Jail
8 Juvenile and Domestic Relations Court
9 City of Charlottesville Courthouse
10 109 E. Jefferson St.
11 Lee Park
12 200 2nd St. N.E.
13 Market St.
14 115 2nd St. N.W.
15 113 W. Market St.
16 115 Second St. N.W.

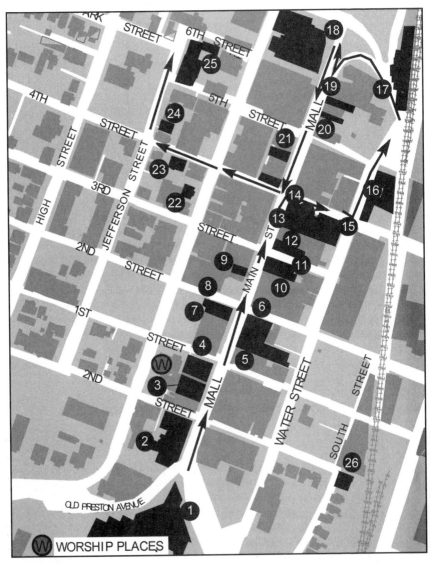

W WORSHIP PLACES

Tour B

1	Omni Hotel	7	123 E. Main	14	322 E. Main	20	510 E. Main
2	223 W. Main	8	Central Place	15	4th.St. S.E. and	21	404 E. Main
3	109 W. Main	9	215 E. Main		Water St.	22	307 E. Market St.
4	105—107 W. Main	10	222 E. Main	16	410 E. Water St.	23	211—215 4th. St N.E
5	110—112 E. Main	11	300 E. Main	17	600 E. Water St.	24	410 E. Jefferson St.
6	114—118 E. Main	12	316 E. Main	18	605 E. Main	25	500 Court Square
		13	320 E. Main	19	520 E. Main	26	200 S.St. West

Tour B

DOWNTOWN & MAIN STREET

The 250-year life of this commercial district has seen a wide range of businesses and services, including grocery, drug, and jewelry stores, restaurants, bars, banks, and cigar factories, makers and sellers of clothing, furniture, carriages, and coffins, and blacksmiths. Just to the west, Main Street passed through "Vinegar Hill," a predominantly African-American business and residential area that was razed in a 1964 urban renewal project (see Tour F). The street followed an early Indian trail that came to be called Three Notch'd Road beginning in the 1740s when the route was marked by trees blazed with three notches from an axe. The road connected Richmond and Tidewater with the Shenandoah Valley of Virginia. In Charlottesville Three Notch'd Road became Main Street and a regional commercial center. To help keep Charlottesville's historic downtown economically viable, in 1976 five blocks of this historic road were closed to traffic and made into the pedestrian Downtown Mall, which was extended two more blocks west in 1981.

Start Tour B on the pedestrian Mall in front of the Omni Charlottesville Hotel. This walk is 12 blocks long. It will take less than one hour. When you reach the other end of the mall you may choose to leave the tour or continue to the Court Square area where Tour A starts.

1 **The Omni Charlottesville Hotel (1987)** The Omni anchors the west end of a seven-block pedestrian mall, which covers part of historic Main Street. Vehicular traffic formerly flowed up the hill to W. Main and on towards the University. A trolley line also operated along Main Street for nearly fifty years, beginning in 1887 with horse-drawn cars, soon converting to an electric line which operated until 1935.

2 **223 West Main Street (1911) and 213 West Main Street (1875)** The facades of these buildings reflect the changing styles of architecture over the years. Compare the simple construction details of the early period 1875 to the more elaborate style of 1911.

*With the hotel at your back, the tour continues east along the Mall for five blocks. Street signs are attached to the light poles. Odd numbered buildings will be on the left or north side of Main St. Even numbered buildings will be on the right or south side. Walk one block. STOP before you cross 2d Street, S.W. Look right to watch for **cars** crossing the Mall. Walk east on the Mall to the middle of the block.*

3 **109 West Main Street (1860)** Over the door on the facade of the brick building are painted signs advertising "Drugs" and "Seeds." For over 60 years Dr. Guy Miller furnished prescriptions, over-the-counter drugs, and goods for farmers. In 1907 the Pure Food and Drug Act eliminated patent medicines—some with as much as 59 percent alcohol. Coincidentally, the same year, Prohibition began locally. Yet drug stores could sell whiskey labeled "for medicinal use only." Tradition says elite Park Street homes (see Tour D) had cupboards fitted to hold weekly "medicine" deliveries.

4 **105—107 West Main Street (1899)** The Leterman Brothers built a six-bay department store, the largest store in Charlottesville. Later, the store was sold and subdivided for a bank, a five and dime, and a shop. From 1920—1982 a family from the local Greek community operated the Brass Rail Restaurant here. Exclusively for men, it provided a shoeshine stand, a hat-cleaning service, billiard tables, and beer dispensed from a mahogany bar.

Continue on the Mall across 1st Street. Go to the middle of the block and stop at the Jefferson Theater on the right (south) side of the street.

5 **110—112 East Main Street (1901, facade 1920)** Occupying a former bank building, the Jefferson Theater offered live theater and motion pictures starting in 1912. Regular theater performances ended in 1929 when "talkies" came to town, but it still hosts occasional concerts and plays, as well as movies.

6 **114—118 East Main Street (1843)** Two adjoining buildings are among the oldest intact buildings on the Mall. The street level of #118 was built to house a jewelry store. The built-in vault still remains. As in years past, today many side doors lead from street level shops to desirable upstairs apartments and offices.

7 **123 East Main Street (1919)** On your left is the town's first skyscraper. Built as Jefferson National Bank it is a reflection of the early 20th-century feeling of prosperity and progress. In 1919 spectators watched as "The Human Fly" scaled this eight-story building. Although the large cornice at the top gave him trouble, he did a handstand atop the narrow ledge to the delight and terror of his audience.

Proceed eastward. As you cross 2d Street, E., look back to the right at the wall that features painted advertisements of the past: "Coca-Cola 5¢" and "Sloans' Liniment."

8 **Central Place (1976)** Central Place is the open area at 2d Street, E. The fountain ahead is reminiscent of the water well once located near here. According to local legend, in 1781 British Colonel Banastre Tarleton quartered some of his troops here. Years later Major James Bankhead quartered men by the well as they assembled for the War of 1812. The three granite stones of the fountain recall the three notches blazed in trees along this early road. The open space is used for musical events and community gatherings.

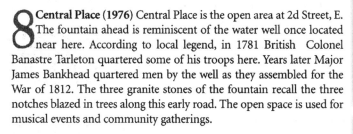

9 **215 East Main Street (1931; closed 1974)** The Paramount Theater with its marquee on the left (north) side of the mall is being restored to its former opulent grandeur. Before the shows patrons admired the 36-foot-high ceilings, ornate murals and gold trim, and satin and velvet furnishings while a theater organ entertained them. The same architects designed the Paramount Theater on

Times Square in New York City. Built during segregation, a side-street door gave access to the 300-seat balcony for black patrons, while 1,000 white patrons sat in the orchestra.

Walk down the Mall to 3d Street, E.

10 **222 East Main Street** The southwest corner was owned in the 1820s by Nancy West, a free black woman. She and her common-law husband David Isaacs were successful merchants and owned considerable commercial property on this road. From 1810 through 1880 the majority of the area's population were people of African heritage, both free and enslaved. A West daughter married the son of Sally Hemings, said to have been fathered by Thomas Jefferson.

Walk across 3d Street, E.

11 **300 East Main Street (1916)** The right (south) side on the corner of this block has a large building with delightful architectural details. Find the Virginia State flower, the dogwood, which the architect added to the neo-classical bank with its imposing Corinthian columns. The banking firm that built this building was founded in 1875. In the first half of the 20th century Charlottesville's Main Street was the financial center of the area. On Main Street seventeen buildings have housed banking institutions at one time or another.

12 **316 East Main Street (1909)** A few steps further along is a building that served as the area's largest hardware store for almost a century. It sold building supplies, housewares, tractors, and, for $359.75 in 1909, a Ford Runabout.

13 **320 East Main Street (1909)** The original name of Gilmore Furniture can still be seen at the top of the building. This building, as well as the one next door, is one city block deep with freight bays opening on Water Street E. The dark squares over the entrance of the copper-fronted doorway are glass turned a deep purple through years of exposure to light.

14 **322 East Main Street (1896)** Timberlake's Drug Store has been in business since 1890. They have been in this location since 1917. Its soda fountain in the rear still offers old-fashioned ammonia Coke.

Leave the Mall, turn right (south) on 4th Street, S.E., and walk down hill to Water Street appropriately named for the creek that once ran through the middle of it.

15 **4th Street S.E. and East Water Streets** You have entered the late 19th-century warehouse, manufacturing, produce distribution, and railroad district. Early in the 20th century a cigar factory and a soda-bottling works were here. The three-story parking structure was built on the site of a "tie lot" where horses and buggies were secured. Three to four blocks west and one block south, you can see large fruit warehouses of the early 1900's and interesting homes on South Street (see "While you are in the neighborhood" at the end of this tour). To the south across the tracks running behind the parking structure is the traditional location for illicit gambling establishments and bordellos. Police finally closed down "Marguerite's" brothel in 1949. When the building was demolished in 1972, many neighbors helped themselves to paper money that had been hidden within the walls.

Do not cross East Water Street, just walk left (east).

16 **410 E. Water Street (1897, 1898 and 1917)** "Charles King & Son Co. Inc. Wholesale Grocery" is painted on the front. By 1915 King's carried everything in the grocery line to supply neighborhood shops—sugar and flour, coffee and candy, spices and tobacco. In 1915 fifteen grocery stores were open on what is now the Downtown Mall. Wholesale deliveries were by horse

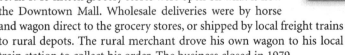

and wagon direct to the grocery stores, or shipped by local freight trains to rural depots. The rural merchant drove his own wagon to his local train station to collect his order. The business closed in 1979.

Walk east one block towards the former train station.

17 **600 East Water Street (1905, 1991)** This elegant building was the passenger and freight station for the
Chesapeake and Ohio Railroad (C&O). A railroad line
running east to west across Virginia first reached
Charlottesville by 1850 and was later absorbed into the C&O.
This line was joined later in the 1850s by a north-south line
which evolved into the Southern Railway, served by Union
Station on W. Main Street at the "junction" where the two railroads crossed (see Tour F, site 7). By 1857 a rail yard was established just east of downtown with a round house and maintenance
shops for steam locomotives, and in the 1880s similar facilities were
built near Union Station. Irish immigrants as well as local men,
including slaves in the early years, provided labor to build and operate the railroads. Changes of crew and engines here meant more resident employees and a boom in the sale of lots in new neighborhoods
such as Fifeville (see Tour F, Oak Lawn) and Belmont (see Tour E, site
15). By 1935 thirty-two passenger trains stopped here daily. In World
War II local soldiers left for training camp from this station.

*Turn left at the corner and stay on the curved sidewalk which follows the
historic route of the Three Notch'd Road. This will take you up to the Mall.
Turn right (east) as you reach the Mall and walk about 100 feet to the brow
of the Amphitheater (1996), a stage for concerts and special events.*

Two miles to the southeast, the lower of the two mountains is the site
of Monticello, Jefferson's home. Across the bridge to the right is
Belmont, a residential area settled by railroad workers (see Tour **E**).

18 **605 East Main Street, City Hall and Annex
(1969, 1990)** City Hall is on your left with a
relief sculpture of James Madison, Thomas
Jefferson, and James Monroe, the three U.S. presidents
who lived nearby. Charlottesville became an independent city in 1888 when land annexed to the town
increased its population to the required 5,000.

Turn around and retrace your steps to the brick Pedestrian Mall.

19 520 East Main Street (1887, 1930) The large lower window served as the door of the horse and trolley barn for the Charlottesville and University Street Railway Co., which began operation in 1887. For a time horse, or mule-drawn and electric-powered trolleys ran side by side from the train depot, down Main Street to the University. Appropriately, the building later became an auto repair shop and gas station.

20 510 East Main Street (1895) Two doors to the west is an example of a Main Street store at the time of the Rotunda fire at the University of Virginia in 1895.

21 404 East Main Street (1915), 415 and 417 (1940) Admire the examples of building trends and architectural fashions on the upper stories of shops on both sides of the street. Compare Arts and Craft style decorations to examples of glass blocks of the Art Moderne rage of the 1940s. The building on the northeast corner of the Mall at 4th Street was erected for a grocery. Residents recall that in the 1930s, when telephones and automobiles were luxuries, this grocer sent his truck each morning to neighborhoods such as the "Woolen Mills" (see Tour E) to collect people's shopping lists. Driver and truck returned the same afternoon with their groceries.

Turn right on 4th Street, N.E., leaving the Mall and walk up hill in a northerly direction. Notice the architectural details on the upper parts of the stores as you pass. After one block STOP before crossing Market Street.

22 307 East Market Street (1853) Look across to the left (west) in the middle of the block to see a fine example of the pilastered Greek Revival style house so popular in Charlottesville in the 1850s. One block east, on December 15, 1806 a dinner was held for the returning Meriwether Lewis and William Clark at the Stone Tavern which later burned.

Cross East Market Street and continue north.

23 211—215 4th Street, N.E. (1830, 1930) In the second block of 4th. St. N.E. are examples of Federal-style townhouses. Note the brick dentil cornice and chimney curtain on No. 215, familiar features on local buildings in the period. These were rental units, and typical of the buildings around Court Square in the 1830s.

Turn right on East Jefferson Street.

24 410 East Jefferson Street (c.1808) The oldest residential building on this tour is the three-window middle section of the townhouses on the right. A window replaced the original doorway many years ago. Adjacent buildings date from the 1820s and later. Look up near the roofline to see the molded brick cornice, now painted white, and also the molded-brick water table at the base of this building.

25 500 Court Square (1926) The ten-story Monticello Hotel opened to serve tourists visiting Monticello. On its roof for a time was the "largest searchlight in the world," visible for 300 miles. Today the former hotel houses apartments and law offices.

Cross the street to the Albemarle County Historical Society Kiosk where Tour A began.

While you are in the neighborhood

26 200 South Street West (1840) 2d Street ends at South Street, the southern boundary of the original town. The yellow house you see was the home of a businessman who founded the Charlottesville and University Street Railway Co. He sold wood and coal from the yard adjacent to his house. These were resources brought in by railroad from West Virginia. The building was used as girls' finishing school and a boarding house, and was restored as an inn (1986).

Tour C

NORTH DOWNTOWN: HIGH, 1ST, AND 2D STREETS

This tour encompasses an area of the City north and northwest of the original commercial center. Its territory includes the northern portion of the original 50-acre grid laid out in 1762 and an area into which the growing community expanded in the early 19th century. By the middle part of the 20th century, North Downtown's popularity as a residential neighborhood had declined greatly, and as population moved into new suburbs, its buildings fell into disrepair. Historic buildings were demolished and residences along High and Park became offices. By 1976 interest had revived and this area was placed under architectural design control. The area was included in the Charlottesville/Albemarle County Courthouse Historic District and the City's first National Register District in 1982. The area covered here is part of the North Downtown Residents Association, one of the City's first neighborhood associations.

Formerly known as Maiden Lane, High Street runs east-west and was added in 1790 to the original 1762 town grid. Residential for most of the history of Charlottesville, the street is now home to offices, law firms, churches, and court buildings.

Begin on West High Street, in front of Christ Church

1 **116 West High Street, Christ Episcopal (1898)** This congregation, initially led by the Reverend Frederick Hatch, began in 1821 and met with the three other major Protestant denominations at the courthouse. The present late-Gothic Revival stone church was built on the site of its wooden 1824 neo-classical predecessor constructed with the aid of parishioner Thomas Jefferson. The present building boasts some beautiful Tiffany stained glass windows, a large rose window, hammer beam interior ceiling, and the city's only carillon, which can be heard throughout downtown Charlottesville when it is played.

2 **104 and 100 West High Street (1891, 1889)** Victorian homes with attractive details including sawn-slat balustrades represent residential construction typical for the late 19th century. No. 104 has an off-center wooden gable, chamfered posts and a pierced frieze. Behind it is a rare original carriage house. The projecting right pavilion of No. 100 originally had a separate recessed entrance and office with a room above. The attractive bracketed veranda has fine sawn-corner brackets.

Cross High Street and turn left (north) onto North 1st Street.

Annexed around 1818 and formerly called "Green Street," North 1st is one of the most interesting streets in Charlottesville for 19th-century residential architecture. The street was developed primarily in the 1880s. In 1890 this and other north-south streets were numbered, centering on this street, and houses were assigned numbers by block for the first time. The numbering of streets and homes was for the convenience of the Postal Service which was launching free home mail delivery. Restorations of several homes on this street in the 1970s marked a return of interest in North Downtown as a residential neighborhood.

3 **422 North 1st Street (1870)** This attractive weatherboard Victorian building is a simple three-bay, two-story frame residence typical of building during Reconstruction. Note its similarity to Nos. 411 and 436.

4 **433 North 1st Street (c.1863)** This cottage Gothic residence, built by Thomas Gilmer, represents one of our few remaining examples of Gothic Revival architecture. The pointed windows, steep central gable, sawn bargeboards, and pendants are characteristic of the style. Gilmer's father, Thomas Walker Gilmer (1802—1844), a local attorney who served as a state delegate and governor, U.S. Congressman, and secretary of the Navy, lived in a house near here from 1836—1844.

5 **504 North 1st Street (c.1873)** This residence has a Colonial Revival veranda and popular post-bellum hip roof covered by tin. The surrounds of the columns are marked by bands of stone "pulled out" to enliven the structure.

6 **521 North 1st Street (c.1859)** An important antebellum Greek Revival residence with four doric pilasters on each facade supporting a handsome cornice with large Italianate cornice brackets, and paired windows with paneled spandrels. The large pilasters link it stylistically to the 1850 Levy Opera House (see Tour **A,** site 4). Banker A. P. Abell, who built the house, was forced by debt to partition the front garden into the present lots of Nos. 514, 518, and 522 across the street, and sold the residence to merchant H. M. Gleason in 1888.

7 **514, 518 and 522 North 1st Street (1889)** These simple two-story clapboard residences, constructed by the same builder, are decorated with gouged floral designs, and have two-story bay windows which were popular at that time.

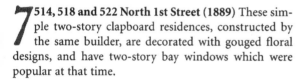

8 **526 North 1st Street (c.1889)** Outstanding example of Victorian vernacular with flush clapboard frieze, bracketed cornice, louvered double circular-headed vents under the gables, spool frieze, and loop balustrade. The house was built by H. M. Gleason for his daughter after he purchased the house across the street. Six levels of lot and garden stretch back to 2d Street.

9 **530 North 1st Street (c.1889)** Finely detailed Victorian vernacular with tripartite stepped-back facade unified by a veranda. The veranda is decorated with a floral motif frieze that is repeated in the pediment over the balcony door, the console brackets, and atop the capitals of the veranda. The house was probably built by Gleason at the time he built No. 526 next door.

Retrace your steps and turn left and descend Hedge Street carefully. At the bottom turn right onto 2d Street, N.E.

10 **426 2d Street, N.E. (c.1836)** This fine example of a late-Federal detached house, built on a characteristic Virginia plan with two stories, a central hall with rooms on either side, and interior end chimneys, was built and occupied by the Lipop family for many years. The brick is laid in Flemish bond with a brick mousetooth cornice. Six-over-six windows are diminished in size in the second story. The squared column porch is a late-19th-century addition.

11 **422 2d Street, N.E., The Old Manse (c.1839)** Very similar in its late Federal styling to the Lipop house next door. The coupled octagonal column porch is original. The building first housed the Charlottesville Female Academy, probably Charlottesville's first girls' school. The school was opened in 1840 by William S. White (1800—1873), second pastor of Charlottesville (First) Presbyterian Church (see tour D, site 6) and chaplain of the University of Virginia, and enrolled 70 students. Before 1863 the house was used as a Baptist manse, and then for many years as the Presbyterian manse, earning it its popular name.

12 **410 2d Street, N.E. (1896)** This is a simplified Queen Anne residence. The style was popular in Charlottesville from 1885—1920. The roof, windows, and doors are original.

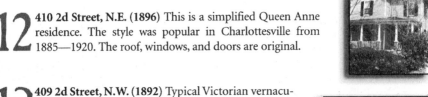

13 **409 2d Street, N.W. (1892)** Typical Victorian vernacular weatherboard house built in 1892. Occupied by members of the Leitch family until 1932.

Turn right onto High Street to view house at 115, then retrace steps east on High Street to 200 block.

14 115 East High Street (2d quarter 19th c.) Representative Federal-style brick residence, typifies a style common in the Court Square area in the second quarter of the 19th century. The front is Flemish bond. The sides in random bond terminate in stepped gables. Originally of unpainted brick, the Doric veranda, rear wing, and single pane sashes are alterations.

15 201 East High Street (c.1835) Neo-classical residence with Georgian forms, altered by the addition of the central gable and overhanging eaves. Dr. Hugh T. Nelson added the west wing and veranda for use as a sanitarium. The veranda's columns are believed to have been moved from the original front entrance portico.

16 205 East High Street (1857—1862) This Italianate residence displays Georgian forms such as a side-hall plan, alongside later Victorian embellishments including a corbeled cornice, octagonal columns, and brackets on the veranda, and two-over-two sashes.

17 211 East High Street (c.1850) Characteristic late-Georgian detached residence. High basement, interior end chimneys and shallow hip roof. The veranda and stucco are not original. The house was the childhood home of art critic, editor, and author S. S. Van Dyne (a pseudonym for Willard Huntington Wright).

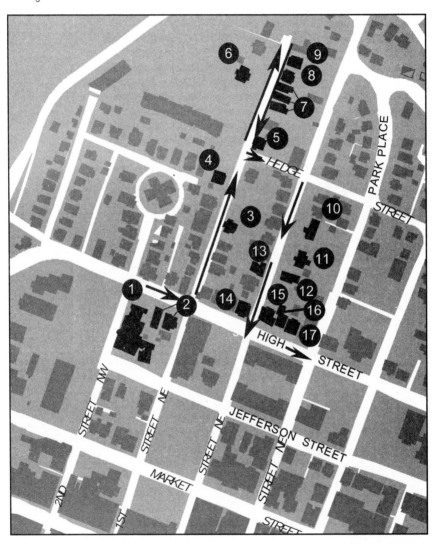

Tour C

1	116 West Main St.	6	521 North 1st. St.	12	410 2d. St., North East
2	104 & 100 West High St.	7	514, 518 & 522 North 1st. St.	13	409 2d. St., North West
3	422 N. 1st. St.	8	526 North 1st. St.	14	115 East High St.
4	433 North 1st. St.	9	530 North 1st. St.	15	201 East High St.
5	504 North 1st. St.	10	426 2d. St., North East	16	205 East High St.
		11	422 2d. St., North East	17	211 East High St.

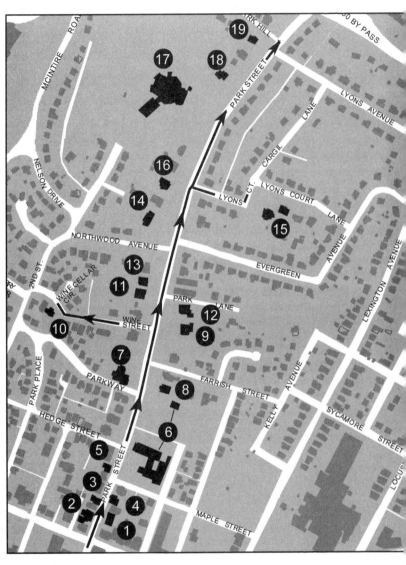

Tour D

1	408—410 Park St.	6	500 Park St.	13	625 Park St.
2	409 Park St.	7	601 Park St.	14	705 Park St.
3	415 Park St.	8	532 Park St.	15	610 Lyons Cou
4	416 Park St.	9	616 Park St.	16	713 Park St.
5	427 Park St.	10	212 Wine St.	17	735 Park St.
		11	621 Park St.	18	743 Park St.
		12	620 Park St.	19	751 Park St.

Tour D

NORTH DOWNTOWN: PARK STREET

Park Street, with its shade trees and grand houses, is one of Charlottesville's most beautiful residential streets and retains much of its 19th-century character. The road winds gently from Court Square to the place that gave the road its name, Cochran's Mill, formerly Park Mill, a part of Dr. George Gilmer's Pen Park estate. By the time of the Civil War Park Street had thirteen houses. In 1874 James Alexander wrote that the "residences on this street are built in good taste, and their situations are lovely and picturesque . . . well calculated for persons of means and leisure." Now, very few buildings in the southernmost two blocks are used as residences, as their proximity to Court Square has made them attractive for law offices and other institutional uses. Looking at the older houses, you will see they grow more dispersed as you travel north, indicating the 19th-century transition from the town to the country.

The southern section of the tour, from Court Square to 610 Lyons Court, can be easily walked, but a car is recommended for the northern sector of the tour and the "While you are in the neighborhood" section. When driving, views of the subject buildings may be unsatisfying if traffic is heavy, but many side streets offer convenient parking or stopping areas from which to view Park Street's houses.

1 **408—410 Park Street, Tower House (c.1854, 1905)** At one time a school for young ladies, the older southern section is also one of the four buildings known to have been used by Federal officers, and perhaps General Philip Sheridan himself, when Charlottesville was occupied by Federal troops in March 1865. This pilastered Italianate building is adorned with an original tower, including double circular-headed windows at its third level, and heavy scrolled brackets at the cornice. The north annex (410 Park Street) was added in 1905.

2 **409 Park Street (1900)** Across the street from the Tower House, this ornate former residence marries a finely detailed pilastered Colonial Revival main block with a Victorian tower. The facade, now painted, is of fine pressed blond brick.

3 **415 Park Street (1814)** One of the oldest houses in the area, this building's bricks were exposed originally. The heavy veranda, stucco, and conical towers with patterned tin roofs were added later as part of a Victorian remodeling.

4 **416 Park Street (1824)** This was constructed in the Federal style with three bays and is similar to other houses built in town in the 1820s. The recessed southern wing, Victorian bay window, and exterior trim probably were added in the mid-19th century.

5 **427 Park Street (1839, 1867)** This building housed a school in the 1850s. Originally, it was built in the Federal style by a merchant tailor's wife as a one-and-a-half-story vernacular residence. Later it was raised to a full two and a half stories, and shortly afterward around 1867, the mansard roof was added giving the residence its Second Empire appearance.

6 **500 Park Street, First Presbyterian Church (1955)** This congregation traces its roots to the South Plains Congregation, which formed in 1819. The regional South Plains Presbyterian Church installed its first pastor, Francis Bowman (1795—1875), in 1824 and constructed its first meeting house in 1827 at the intersection of Market Street and 2d Street, N.E., where its successors, known respectively as Charlottesville Presbyterian Church and First Presbyterian Church, made their homes until 1955. The neo-Georgian church, modeled on London, England's St. Martin-in-the-Fields, was built on the site of three large 19th-century residences. The driveway on the north end of the property leads to the restored carriage house of one of the houses formerly located on this site.

7 601 **Park Street (1891)** Charlottesville's Mayor J. Samuel McCue (1861—1905) built this residence. In 1904, his wife was murdered in this house while bathing upstairs. McCue was convicted in a sensational trial that received national press coverage. His execution at the nearby County Jail (see Tour A, site 7) took place before the unsuccessful conclusion of his appeal, and was the last legal public hanging in Virginia. The house is now called "Comyn Hall," named for an earlier and even more striking nearby Park Street mansion no longer standing.

8 532 **Park Street (c.1850s, 1920)** This house was occupied from 1855—1884 by attorney Shelton F. Leake (1812—1884). During his political career, Leake was a delegate (1842—1843), the state's first lieutenant governor (1851), and twice a congressman (1845—1847, 1859—1861). In 1920 this house was completely remodeled to its present Colonial Revival form. Its original appearance is unknown.

9 616 **Park Street (1884)** Built by the City's first Judge, R. T. W. Duke, Jr. (1853—1926), this asymmetrical white frame Queen Anne house designed by architect S. R. Burrage Reed of New York, features a veranda with turned Victorian columns and a porch gazebo. It remained in the Duke family until the late 20th century, and has changed little in its appearance.

Turn left off Park Street onto Wine Street.

Formerly an alley, Wine Street still has the feel of a country lane, but is embellished by several bungalow-style homes dating from the street's residential development in the early 20th century.

10 212 **Wine Street, Monticello Wine Co. House (1884)** This house was built for the superintendent of the Monticello Wine Co. which won several prizes in international wine competitions in Paris. Since Jefferson's time, vineyards have been operated in Albemarle County. In the late 19th century Charlottesville claimed to be the capital of the Virginia Wine Belt, and the area's most successful vineyard was centered here. Vines grew on 2.6 surrounding acres and a wine cellar was located to the west across 2d Street. Prohibition killed the business in 1914, but in recent years fine vineyards have returned to central Virginia. The house was built to face south, not north onto Wine Street. The front still can be viewed partially from either side of 307 Parkway on the south side of the block.

After visiting the Monticello Wine Co. House, retrace your path back to Park Street to resume this tour. (Alternatively, you may continue down the hill and turn left onto 2d Street to pick up Tour C at site 11 or take an immediate right onto Perry and left on McIntire to view Transfiguration of our Savior Church—see "While you are in the neighborhood"—and pick up Tour F and follow it in reverse.) Turn left onto Park Street.

11 **621 Park Street, Northwood (1843)** Northwood, a Colonial Revival house was constructed by renowned University of Virginia law Professor John Barbee Minor (1813—1895). Minor was one of the leading legal minds of 19th-century America. He influenced thinking on secession, on the voting rights compromises of Reconstruction, and he helped draft Virginia's first legislation establishing free public schools. Of all the University's faculty in the 1880's, Minor was considered by his student, Woodrow Wilson, to be the most impressive.

12 **620 Park Street (1894; National Register)** This significant late Victorian residence was constructed in 1897 in the Queen Anne style by builder William T. Vandegrift. Its second owner was philanthropist William J. Rucker (d. 1941), who left it to the Martha Jefferson Hospital. It was used in 1950s and 1960s as a rooming house. One of the roomers in the 1950s is believed to have been future U.S. Supreme Court Justice Sandra Day O'Conner, who lived here with her husband while he was a student at the Judge Advocate General's School. The house was restored in the 1970s and 1980s.

13 **625 Park Street (1902)** This residence, with an attractive Colonial Revival Doric paired column portico, was designed by Washington architect Alfred B. Mullett, who also designed the Old Executive Office Building near the White House.

14 **705 Park Street (1859; National Register)** The first owner, Judge William Joseph Robertson (1817—1889), served as the County's Commonwealth Attorney in 1850s and sat on the Virginia Supreme Court from 1859 until the Civil War. Union victory ended his judgeship, but he went on to become in 1888 the first president of the Virginia Bar Association. This Italianate building is considered one of the finest antebellum structures downtown. Two gabled pavilions shelter an entrance bay with a balcony supported by massive scrolled brackets. Notice the scalloped, cyprus hoods over the windows, the brackets at the peaks and ends of the gables, the stucco scored to imitate masonry and the clustered chimneys.

Turn right onto Lyons Court. Drive down Lyons Court to see the next site better, then turn around in front of it and come back to Park St.

Lyons Court and Lyons Court Lane took their names from the second owner of 610 Lyons Court, Judge Thomas Barton Lyons, who is not believed to have practiced law locally.

15 **610 Lyons Court (1858)** This beautiful Greek Revival home, now named Bonahora for the ship that brought John Jefferson to America in 1619, features brick pilasters, dual windows, and a tripartite window. The porch with Ionic columns was added in 1890. The house has a 4,000 gallon water tank in the attic, suggesting that it was the first Charlottesville residence with indoor plumbing. An elderly resident even recalled seeing men working with a pump rigged like a see-saw. The house behind and left of Bonahora, 706 Lyons Court Lane, formerly was its carriage house.

Return to Park Street and prepare to turn right (north). Before you turn, pause and look across Park Street and slightly to the left at the next site, 713 Park Street.

16 **713 Park Street (1861)** This brick home was built by Judge Egbert R. Watson, who resided here until his death in 1887. From 1919 through 1971 it was owned by Christ Episcopal Church (see tour C, site 2) and used as its manse or rectory. It gracefully blends Italianate details such as arched windows, peaked gables, and large brackets under overhanging eaves, with late Georgian massing.

17 **735 Park Street, First Baptist Church (Main Street) (1970s)** Baptists first began meeting in this area around 1767, and had a meeting house in the area of the University in 1773. This congregation began informally around 1820 and worshiped at the courthouse with the Episcopalians, Presbyterians, and Methodists. In 1831 Reuben Coleman and James Goss, students at the University, formally started the new church and served as its first ministers. Coleman was pastor until 1837. John A. Broadus, pastor from 1851 to 1859, later became president of the Southern Baptist Convention. Four other Baptist congregations ultimately sprang from this one: High Street Baptist, now University Baptist (see Tour G, site 3), Delavan Baptist now First Baptist Main Street (see Tour F, site 6), Belmont Baptist, and Jefferson Park Baptist.

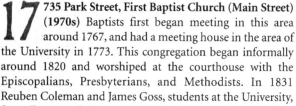

18 **743 Park Street (1892)** This asymmetrical house is an outstanding example of the Victorian Shingle style popular in the 1880s and 1890s. It is built of field stone and clapboard. The gabled veranda is framed by an octagonal tower and a lower round tower.

19 **751 Park Street (1904)** This house is a fine example of the Colonial Revival style which was very popular at the turn of the century. It is the only frame example of that style on Park Street.

The next three sites may be viewed as you follow Park Street North. The first one is on a side street.

While you are in the neighborhood

• **603—605 Watson Avenue, Enderly (1859)** When built, Enderly was a country estate. A winter kitchen and dining room were on the basement level of the main house, where the half windows are easily visible below the large full width porch. The house next door, 605 Watson, was its summer kitchen and servant's quarters.

• **1105 Park St., Hard Bargain (1878)** This two story frame house built in the Homestead style has an attractive bay window. Notice also the finely detailed woodwork in the gable of the outbuilding to the left of the main house.

Cochran's Mill is located on a bend that is particularly dangerous due to traffic. Follow Park Street north until you cross a small bridge across Meadow Creek where Park Street becomes Rio Road. Immediately after passing a duplex on your right, you will see a small white house on the right nestled almost into the hillside below the road. Take an immediate left onto Brookway Drive, park and walk a few steps back to the street to view the house.

• **435 East Rio Road, Cochran's Mill house (1754)** Both the well-preserved colonial house and mill were built in 1754, and were part of Dr. George Gilmer's Pen Park estate. The mill is closest to the road, with its roof barely visible just to the right of the driveway. Gilmer was a leading patriot, who as a lieutenant in the Albemarle Volunteers twice led local militia to Williamsburg against Governor Dunmore in 1775. The troops turned back, but Gilmer's status as a leader did not suffer. By 1800, the site was known as Park Mill but was renamed Cochran's Mill for a new owner in 1829. For generations, a pond here was a popular location for skating.

See directions following site 10.

• **100 Perry Drive, Church of the Transfiguration of Christ Our Lord (Metamorphosis Soteros), Greek Orthodox (1954)** Since its completion, the Greek Orthodox Church has been the center of one of Charlottesville's most vibrant immigrant communities. The first Greek immigrant arrived here in 1903. Attracted by the opportunity to establish their own businesses, Greek immigrants have been active entrepreneurs throughout the 20th century.

Tour E

EASTERN CHARLOTTESVILLE—
WOOLEN MILLS—BELMONT

This driving tour encompasses the eastern section of downtown Charlottesville and the area around the Woolen Mills—a working-class neighborhood that grew up at the confluence of Moore's Creek and the Rivanna River. Additionally, two historic structures are included in the Belmont section of Charlottesville—southeast of downtown—as well as a beautiful home to the northeast.

The tour begins at Maplewood Cemetery just north of the downtown mall, at the corner of Lexington Avenue and Maple Street. There are entrances to the cemetery on both of these roads.

1 **Maplewood Cemetery (1831)** One of Charlottesville's oldest cemeteries, many of Maplewood's slumbering denizens led fascinating lives. Some of the most interesting include: local boy-made-good and city benefactor Paul Goodloe McIntire (1860—1952); Benjamin Franklin Ficklin, one of the founders of the Pony Express (1827—1871); Lettitia Cox Shelby (1723—1777), the mother of Isaac Shelby, Kentucky's first governor; and two Confederate generals—John Marshall Jones, who was killed at the Battle of the Wilderness leading the famed "Stonewall Brigade" (1821—1864), and Armistead Lindsay Long, Robert E. Lee's military secretary and biographer (1825—1891).

From Maplewood take Lexington Avenue south to E. High Street. Merge right onto E. High and travel one block. Note that the road changes to 9th Street. Turn right on E. Jefferson Street and travel one block. 802 E. Jefferson is on the left at the first corner.

2 **802 E. Jefferson Street (1820)** Constructed by Dr. Charles Carter, this beautiful three-story Federal townhouse is typical of the style popular during the nation's early years. The home's features include wooden lintels with corner blocks and a transom over the entrance. The bottom two stories were laid in Flemish Bond, while the third story—obviously a later addition—was set in American Bond.

From 802 E. Jefferson turn south, left, onto 8th Street and after one block take a left onto Market. Follow E. Market Street for approximately one mile.

3 **E. Market Street** This mile-long straight stretch of road was originally constructed in the early 1830s as part of the Blue Ridge and Rivanna Turnpike that connected the Rivanna River (east of Charlottesville) and the village of Brooksville in western Albemarle County. Closely paralleling it to the south was the old Three Notch'd (or Three Chopt) Road. Hacked through the center of the county in the early 1740s, the Three Notch'd Road was one of Central Virginia's first important thoroughfares.

Continue on E. Market until you reach its intersection with Riverside Street (where you will notice a charming wooden chapel to your left). Park in this immediate vicinity, where spaces are often available curbside.

4 **The Woolen Mills Neighborhood** Welcome to the Woolen Mills neighborhood, built on the rise of land at the confluence of two watercourses—Moore's Creek and the Rivanna River. This area once served as an important Central Virginia transportation nexus, featuring: the Rivanna crossing known as Secretary's Ford (c.1740s), named for Col. John Carter, the Colonial Secretary under King George II of England; the head of Rivanna navigation, Charlottesville's port (c.1815)—called "Pireus" after the port of Athens, since early Charlottesvillians fancied their town "the Athens of the South"; the county's first wooden toll-bridge (1826); and the Virginia Central Railroad bridge (1848). Spurred on by the growth of the "Charlottesville Woolen Mills" (see below), the Woolen Mills neighborhood grew dramatically in the 1880s and 1890s. What started as a working-class neighborhood apart from Charlottesville, spread steadily to the west, eventually connecting itself to the city.

5 **The Woolen Mills** The Charlottesville Woolen Mills was founded in 1867, but mills of various types—powered by the Rivanna River—had been in operation on this site since 1795. Prior to the Civil War the mills here produced rough material for slave garments. During the conflict they manufactured cloth for Confederate uniforms. Later specialization in fine, military-style fabrics won national recognition for the firm. At its height the company was reportedly supplying 90 percent of the country's military academies, including West Point.

The Charlottesville Woolen Mills closed in 1964, but from the 1890s until just after World War II the company was one of Central Virginia's largest industries. A few important old structures associated with the Woolen Mills can still be seen along the last few blocks of E. Market Street. The mill's brick office building (1915 E. Market), for example, now serves as a condominium.

6 **The Woolen Mills Chapel (1887)** On the corner of E. Market and Riverside Streets the chapel was constructed in response to a religious fervor that swept through the Woolen Mills community in 1886. This white clapboard non-denominational chapel was funded by a public subscription of the mill workers. It was consecrated on 13 May 1888. In 1908 the building was more than doubled in size with the addition of Sunday School classrooms to the west side of the sanctuary. A typical example of late-19th-century vernacular church construction, the chapel features: pointed Gothic doors, windows, and shutters; a steeply pitched gable roof; and a beautiful 50-foot octagonal Victorian spire. The steeple bell still rings each Sunday to call the service.

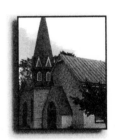

7 **1901 E. Market Street (c. late 1830s)** This small brick building is known as "Woolen Mills Cottage," "Pireus Store," and "The Woolen Mills Tavern." It became a company store in the 1850s and was later used as factory-owned housing.

8 **1907—1908, 1909—1910, 1911—1912 E. Market Street (1881)** Alongside "Pireus Store" these three duplexes were constructed by the Charlottesville Woolen Mills as housing for its laborers. The quaint brick cottages feature double-gabled roofs.

Take Riverside Street north and travel one block to the intersection with Chesapeake Street. Turn into the park on the right.

9 **Riverview Park—Riverside and Chesapeake Streets (1993)** Part of Charlottesville's Greenbelt Trail System, Riverview Park is a great way to experience the beautiful Rivanna River. From the parking lot a scenic riverside trail runs for approximately 1.3 miles to the U.S. Route 250 Bypass at Free Bridge. On any given afternoon visitors to Riverview will likely encounter Charlottesvillians jogging, biking, power-walking, and fishing along the river's tree-lined banks. The trail is also a big favorite of dogs and their human companions. Completely accessible to persons with disabilities, the park and trail are open every day from 7 a.m. until dark.

Drive two blocks west on Chesapeake Street. The entrance to Riverview Cemetery is at the intersection of Chesapeake and Riverview.

10 **Riverview Cemetery—Chesapeake and Riverview Streets (1892)** Overlooking a broad loop of the Rivanna, Riverview is the final resting place of many of Charlottesville's prosperous Greek community members. Here, too, was buried Henry Clay Marchant (1838—1910), who managed the nearby Charlottesville Woolen Mills from 1867 until his death. Riverview also contains the remains of two Revolutionary War soldiers: Nicholas Lewis (1734—1808), the grandfather of Meriwether Lewis of Lewis and Clark fame; Thomas Walker Lewis (1763—1807); and, beneath the tall obelisk, Confederate General Thomas Lafayette Rosser (1836—1910), who, while commanding Southern cavalry in the Shenandoah in 1864, was given the nickname "Savior of the Valley."

From the cemetery's highest point look to the southeast for a an excellent view of Monticello. From Riverview take Chesapeake Street west for three blocks to Meade Avenue. Turn right and take the first left onto E. Jefferson Street. Two blocks west turn right onto 12th Street.

11 **1201 E. Jefferson Street (1825—1827)** Known as "The Farm," this home was built by U.Va. Professor John A. G. Davis (1801—1840) who was tragically murdered by a student from Georgia. Laid all around in Flemish Bond, this home shows the influence of Jefferson's neo-classical tastes. The features include a Federal-style doorway with fanlight and carved keystone; coupled Tuscan entranceway columns and entablature; and, reminiscent of Monticello's terrace-walks, a Chinese trellis

over the portico. Interestingly, this home was used as a headquarters by General George Armstrong Custer (1839—1876), a West Point friend of General Rosser's during the Federal occupation of Charlottesville, 3—6 March 1865.

Sitting alongside "The Farm" is another of Charlottesville's historically important homes.

12 **309 12th Street (c.1770)** This painted-brick, vernacular cottage is the second structure built on this site by Nicholas Lewis (1734—1808). Its large, buttressed chimney is typical of early Virginia homes. The cornice is decorated with brick modillions extending from the walls. The east elevation's large dormers and French windows are later "unsympathetic" additions. This earlier version of "The Farm" was used as a headquarters 4—5 June 1781 by British Colonel Banastre Tarleton when he captured Charlottesville—then serving temporarily as Virginia's capital. Interesting to note that, ironically, these adjacent homes were used by two of Virginia's most infamous invading cavalrymen.

Return to E. Jefferson and turn right, west. A short hop of three blocks will bring you to 9th Street. The next stop is on the corner, to the right.

13 **901 E. Jefferson Street (1806—1807)** After its original construction this large, rambling home was added to in 1884 and 1907. The last, a two-story, five-bay addition in six-course American Bond was put up across the southern, E. Jefferson, facade including: a two-story portico with four columns on the first level topped by Tuscan, Colonial Revival columns on the second; a double entrance with sidelights and rectangular transom; and double-sash windows.

While you are in the neighborhood

From the intersection of E. Jefferson and 9th streets, turn left onto 9th, cross the bridge over the railroad tracks and, three blocks later, turn left onto Belmont Avenue. The first stop is in the middle of the second block.

14 **The Belmont Neighborhood** Welcome to Belmont, a working-class neighborhood that grew up in the late 1880s and early 1890s as housing for Charlottesville's many railroad and industrial workers.

15 **759 Belmont Avenue (c.1837)** The neighborhood takes its name from this home, erected on the area's highest point. "Belmont" is an unusually large, brick seven-bay two-story example of Late Georgian architecture. (A modern addition faces Belmont Avenue: the original front is best viewed from the church parking lot accessed around the corner on Church Street.) The original building features nine-over-nine windows on the main floor, with jack arches above them; six-over-six windows on the second story, which almost meet the deep, wooden cornice under the roof line; and chimneys flush with the end walls. The Greek Revival door frame features shouldered architrave trim.

Drive east on Belmont Avenue, cross Monticello Road, and turn left and then right onto Bainbridge Street. Turn right onto Carleton Avenue and travel two blocks, across the intersection with Carleton Road.

16 **1102 Carleton Avenue (1916)** Known as the "Young Building," this two-story brick structure was constructed by the J. S. Young Co. It is the city's only example of Flemish architecture expressed with large, curving Jacobean gables. Other features include segmental and jack arches; small, decorative brick quoins; and the company's monogram above the entrance.

To reach the home below, retrace your route back across the bridge over the railroad and along 9th Street. After two blocks 9th veers to the right and becomes East High Street. One block later turn left (north) onto Locust Ave. and travel two and one-half blocks. Look for number 819 on the right.

• **818 Locust Avenue (1840)** Known as "Locust Grove" this 2-story brick house exhibits simple Greek Revival details. An 18th century house on this site—built by Thomas W. Lewis on land given him by his father, Nicholas Lewis of "The Farm"—had burned before George Sinclair purchased the 534-acre estate in 1839. The property was subdivided in the 1890s. Locust Grove's summer kitchen and smokehouse are still standing.

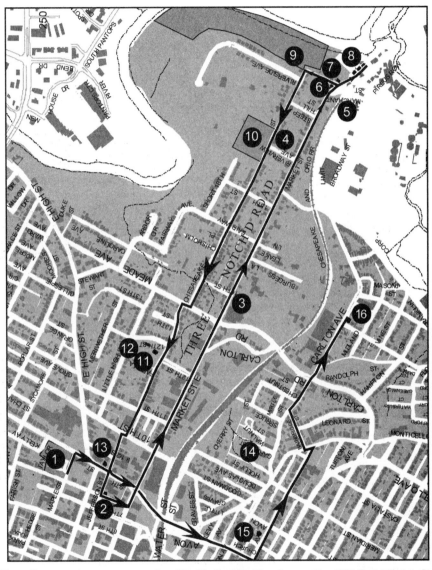

Tour E

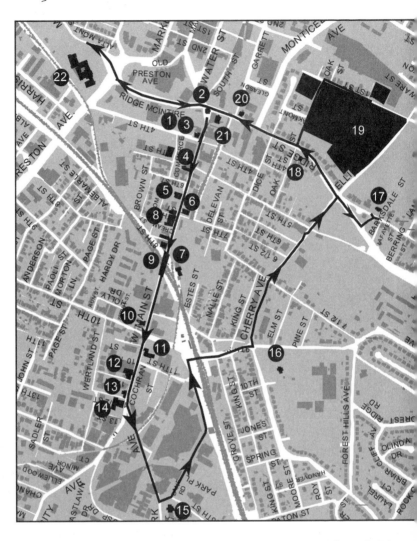

Tour F

1 Jefferson High School

2 Lewis and Clark Statue

3 333 West Main St.

4 503 West Main St.

5 617—619 W. Main St.,
  Hotel Gleason

6 632 West Main St.
  First Baptist Church

7 810 West Main St.
  Union Station

8 633-817 West Main St.

9 Drewary Brown Bridge

10 909 West Main St.

11 1022 West Main St.

12 1111, 1113 West Main St.

13 1211, 1215 West Main St.

14 University Baptist Church

15 1404 Jefferson Park Ave.

16 501 9th. South West, Oak L

17 632 Ridge St.

18 505 Ridge St.

19 Oakwood, Zion, and Hebrew
   Cemeteries

20 204 Ridge St.

21 Mt. Zion Baptist Church

22 401 McIntire Rd.

Tour F

WEST MAIN STREET / RIDGE STREET DRIVING TOUR

This 3-mile tour is too long to be walked in its entirety, but parking is available along the route so that short segments could be walked.

The tour begins in the parking lot between Ridge-McIntire Road and 4th Street, N.W. This is Vinegar Hill, the site of Charlottesville's first urban renewal project in the mid-1960s. At that time, this was an African-American residential neighborhood with a mixture of rental and owner-occupied houses. Zion Union Baptist Church stood on a bluff above 4th Street. A creek known as Schenk's Branch ran through the neighborhood. Most of the late 19th-century commercial buildings along W. Main Street housed African-American-owned businesses. (See the state historical marker on W. Main Street in front of the Omni Hotel.) The name "Vinegar Hill" goes back at least 150 years, and its origins are uncertain.

1 **Corner of 4th and Commerce streets, Jefferson High School (1926—1967)** Across 4th Street from the parking lot and facing south on Commerce Street is Jefferson High School, the first public high school for African-Americans in the city. The city first instituted public schooling, both for blacks and for whites, in the 1870s. After Jackson P. Burley High School on Rose Hill Drive opened in 1951, this became Jefferson Elementary School, and was enlarged several times over the years. It closed in 1964.

Exit the parking lot, turning right (south) onto Ridge-McIntire, then turn right onto W. Main Street.

West Main Street follows the route of the old Three Notch'd Road, constructed in the 1730s by improving an old Indian trail to provide a route between Richmond and the Shenandoah Valley. This stretch between Charlottesville and the University remained a rural road until well into the 19th century. The establishment of Union Station in 1885 at the intersection of two railroad lines three blocks west of here spurred the opening of inns and hotels. In the early 20th century, these were joined by service stations and automobile dealers. The area suffered a period of decline in the last half of the century when rail travel diminished.

2 **W. Main Street and Ridge-McIntire—Lewis and Clark Statue** The statue in the middle of the intersection is by Charles Keck and commemorates the 1803—1806 Lewis and Clark Expedition. The three figures are Albemarle County native Meriwether Lewis, William Clark, and Sacajawea, the Shoshone woman who served as their guide. Local philanthropist Paul Goodloe McIntire commissioned the statue in 1919.

3 **333 W. Main Street (1820, 1833—1840)** The oldest remaining building on the Three Notch'd Road between Charlottesville and the University, this house consists of two Federal side-hall-plan townhouses, the eastern one built in 1820 and the western, c.1833-1840. Despite many alterations over the years, their Flemish bond brickwork, stepped gables, and mouse-

tooth cornice remain. George P. Inge, an African-American schoolteacher and chairman of the local Republican Party, established a grocery store on the main floor in 1890, and it was continued by his son until 1979. The family originally lived above the store, and George Inge's Hampton Institute classmate, Booker T. Washington, was often their guest there.

4 **503 W. Main Street (1824)** With its Flemish bond brickwork, mousetooth cornice, curtain wall between the chimneys, and side-hall floor plan, this house is representative of the more substantial houses in the Federal style built by prosperous members of the community in the early decades of the 19th century. The Colonial Revival veranda is a 1911 addition.

5 **617—619 W. Main Street, Hotel Gleason/Albemarle (1896)**
This is the last survivor of the many inns and hotels that once stood along the road between downtown Charlottesville and U.Va. Built in 1896 as the Hotel Gleason and enlarged c.1911—1913, it was the city's premier hotel for a quarter century. Renamed the Albemarle Hotel in the 1930s, it continued in operation until the mid-1970s. The recessed loggia with four Corinthian columns once held rocking chairs for hotel guests. A small second-story portico-in-antis has a Palladian window and an elaborate pressed metal entablature.

6 **632 W. Main Street, First Baptist Church (1877—1884)** In 1864, 800 African-American members of the Charlottesville Baptist Church withdrew to organize a new church. Four years later, they purchased the old Delavan Hotel, which had served as a Civil War hospital and later as a free school for African-American children. They initially took its name for their church. The present Victorian Romanesque style building was begun in 1877 and completed in 1884. It is still occupied by the congregation, and, like its parent church, is called First Baptist.

Turn left onto 7th Street, S.W., at the light next to the church, then right into the railroad station parking lot.

7 **810 W. Main Street Union Station (1885, c.1915)** Union Station was built in 1885 at the junction of the north-south (Southern Railroad) and east-west (C&O) lines. It was enlarged and remodeled in the 1913—1918 period. For over half a century this would have been the point of arrival for most travelers and their first sight of Charlottesville. In its heyday, there was a tea room on the upper level and an elevated covered walkway over the tracks to W. Main Street. After decades of deterioration with the decline in rail travel, restoration was begun in 1998.

Return to W. Main Street and continue west.

8 **633—817 W. Main Street** Most of these commercial buildings date from the late 19th and early 20th centuries. All are vernacular with some Victorian details. The building at 711 W. Main Street has a metal-clad facade that matches that of the Anderson Building on the University Corner (see Tour G, site 8).

9 **Drewary Brown Bridge** When the railroad bridge was rebuilt in 1998, it was named in honor of respected local African-American civil rights leader Drewary Brown (1918—1998), a man who in his lifetime worked to build bridges between different segments of the community.

10 **909 W. Main Street (1850s, 1935)** Built in the 1850s, this vernacular house with simple Greek Revival details and a corbeled brick cornice with brick dentils, is representative of a form that remained popular here up until the Civil War. The building was extended to the rear in 1935, and the porte cochere and Colonial Revival veranda are also 20th-century additions.

11 **1022 W. Main Street (1907)** This handsome Jeffersonian Revival house with a full-height Tuscan portico was built in 1907 by John S. Patton, who was later librarian at U.Va. It was adapted for use as a bank in 1954.

At this point, the tour overlaps the University Corner Walking Tour (Tour G) for a short distance.

12 **1111, 1113 W. Main Street (1823, 1839)** The eastern of these two fine Federal side-hall-plan townhouses, 1111, has a wooden cornice with modillions and egg-and-dart moulding. It is probably the earlier, built in 1823. Its construction is attributed to James Dinsmore, one of Jefferson's master builders at the University and a former owner of the property, but the sec-

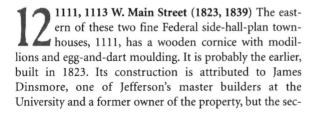

ond house, 1113, was apparently built after Dinsmore's 1830 death. It has parapet gables, a mousetooth cornice, and a fine fish-eye transom above narrow paired entrance doors. The small entrance porches are not original. A brick dependency adjacent to 12th Street, probably a kitchen with servants' quarters above, survives.

13 **1211, 1215 W. Main Street (1826, mid-1800s)** This handsome Federal townhouse was built in 1826 on land purchased from Jefferson's master builder James Dinsmore, and construction is attributed to him. It has Flemish bond brickwork, a mousetooth cornice, stepped gables with an attic thermal window, and delicate fanlight and sidelights at the entrance. The small entrance portico and two-story enclosed side porch are 20th-century additions. From 1838 to 1913 this house was occupied by the family of Clement P. McKennie (1798—1856), who, with his brother, published Charlottesville's first newspaper in 1820. The building to the west, the "Annex," was probably built in the mid-1800s and may have been used as student housing.

14 **1223 W. Main Street University Baptist Church (1928—1929)** This large impressive church has its origins in the High Street Baptist Church built in 1901. In the 1920s the congregation decided to relocate here, closer to the University, in order to provide a house of worship for students. The six-columned brick church was designed by Richmond-based architect Herbert Levi Cain.

Turn left onto Jefferson Park Avenue at the light in front of the church. Here the tour leaves the route of the Three Notch'd Road and follows Wheeler's Road, another early route. It passes under the railroad tracks and between the 1960 and 1985 buildings of the University Hospital. Just after you pass under the second of two large, enclosed walkways, a large Victorian house will be visible on a hill to the left. Turn left, just before it, onto Lane Road.

15 **1404 Jefferson Park Avenue (1896)** This imposing house with its picturesque roofline, octagonal tower, porte cochere, ornate chimneys, and elaborate Romanesque Revival entrance was the home of Dr. Paul W. Barringer (1857—1941). As professor of medicine and chairman of the faculty at U.Va., he was the driving force behind the establishment of the University Hospital in 1901. Among the guests of the University whom the Barringers entertained here were William Jennings Bryan in 1897 and President Theodore Roosevelt in 1903. The house was restored in 1985.

Follow Lane Road to the left behind the 1985 hospital building, then left onto Crispell Drive to the 9th-10th streets connector.

Sally Hemings's son Madison Hemings owned property in this area, and she is believed to have spent her last years here after leaving Monticello. No buildings remain from that time. Several blocks west of here, across Jefferson Park Avenue from New Cabell Hall, archeological research has been done at the 1833 house site and graveyard of the family of Kitty Foster, a free African-American woman.

Turn right (south) onto the 9th-10th streets connector and cross Cherry Avenue, where the street becomes 9th Street, S.W.

This neighborhood is Fifeville. Visible on the right, up a long private driveway, is Oak Lawn. On-street parking affords a view of the house.

16 501 9th Street, S.W., Oak Lawn (1822) This was the first building in Charlottesville to receive an individual listing on the National Register of Historic Places. Its form is that of the Palladian villa, with a two-story pedimented central block flanked by one-story side pavilions. Its Tuscan portico and Flemish bond brickwork are further examples of the Federal style. It was built in 1822 by Colonel Nimrod Bramham, a Court Square merchant. Construction is attributed to James Dinsmore, an Irish carpenter brought to the area by Thomas Jefferson. Oak Lawn has been in the Fife family since 1847 and was meticulously restored in 1998. It was originally surrounded by a plantation of 338 acres, nearly all of which has now been subdivided. Bramham and Fife graveyards are located south of the house.

Return to Cherry Avenue and turn right (east). Continue to the traffic light at the top of the hill, at the intersection with Ridge Street.

Ridge Street was once one of the most fashionable residential streets in the city, the home of prosperous merchants and businessmen. It was a racially integrated neighborhood from the very beginning, with several free African-American families owning homes there and on Lankford Avenue in the 1840s and 1850s. After the Civil War, more African-Americans built houses at the far southern end of the street. In the mid-1900s many houses were divided into apartments or demolished. The realignment of Ridge with 5th Street in 1973 cut the neighborhood in two and caused the destruction of eleven more houses, some dating to the early 1840s.

At the traffic light, turn right onto Ridge Street, and immediately turn left onto a small access road leading to the disconnected southern end of Ridge Street. Immediately in front of you will be #17.

17 **632 Ridge Street, Albemarle Military Institute (1854)** This vernacular house with Greek Revival details is the only survivor of the Albemarle Military Institute, operated by Colonel John Bowie Strange (1823—1862) from 1856 until the beginning of the Civil War. Strange was killed at the Battle of Boonesboro while leading a local infantry regiment, and the school never re-opened. The house is believed to have been designed and built by central Virginia's master brickmason William B. Phillips. The entrance door with sidelights and rectangular transom and the flat-roofed portico are typical of the Greek Revival style.

Retrace your steps to Ridge Street, turn right, and continue straight through the traffic light.

Most of the remaining houses on this section of Ridge Street were built between 1870 and 1920 and are vernacular buildings with either Victorian or Colonial Revival details.

18 **505 Ridge Street (c.1845)** This house has the stepped gables, Flemish bond brickwork, mousetooth cornice, and lintels with corner blocks typical of the Federal style. Its fine entrance features sidelights, transom, and fluted pilasters. The entrance porch is not original. Although its style is more typical of the

1820s, tax records indicate that it was built c.1845, which still makes it one of the earliest remaining on the street.

Turn right onto Oak Street.

19 **Oakwood, Zion, and Hebrew Cemeteries** Three cemeteries are located one block east of Ridge Street. The large cemetery on the right is Oakwood, a public cemetery established in the early 1860s. On the left is Zion cemetery, a small, old, African-American cemetery. Hebrew Cemetery is located east of Oakwood Cemetery, across South 1st Street.

Return to Ridge Street and turn right (north).

20 **204 Ridge Street (1862)** This is one of only three or four true Gothic Revival cottages in the city. The walls are covered with the original rusticated wooden siding. The delicately undulating sawnwork gable trim is unique. Later additions have filled in the rear corners of the originally T-shaped structure, and several street widenings have made its English basement less usable. The present veranda replaced the original one-bay entrance porch in 1923. A nicely detailed dependency also survives.

21 **105 Ridge Street Mt. Zion Baptist Church (1883—1884)** Mt. Zion Baptist Church was organized in 1867 by a group of the 800 African-American members of the Charlottesville Baptist Church who had withdrawn their membership in 1864. The present Romanesque Revival building was erected in 1883—1884, replacing a smaller wooden church building. It was designed and built by Ridge Street resident G. Wallace Spooner, whose father had been one of Jefferson's builders at U.Va. The steeple and the stained glass windows were completed in the 1890s. The octagonal lantern atop the entrance tower was originally wooden shingled and had eight pedimented window vents.

Follow Ridge Street north across W. Main Street, down the hill past this tour's starting point, and across Preston Avenue. The street becomes McIntire Road at this point.

22 **401 McIntire Road Lane High School (1940)** Lane High School opened in 1940, replacing the old Midway High School (which had been re-named in 1924 in honor of former principal James W. Lane) as the city's high school for white students. Pendleton Clark of Lynchburg was the architect. Lane was closed for the 1958 fall semester under Virginia's "Massive Resistance" anti-integration laws. It re-opened for the spring semester and was desegregated without incident in September 1959. It was replaced by Charlottesville High School in 1974 and was sold to Albemarle County and extensively remodeled for use as the county office building.

Tour G

THE CORNER TOUR

This tour will guide you through the University Corner district, concluding at the University of Virginia Rotunda. "The Corner" is the local name for the five-block commercial district across the street from the University of Virginia.

The phrase "the Corner" was first used in the early 1900s by University students and referred to the sparse collection of stores and businesses at the intersection of University Avenue and the entrance to the University Grounds—once literally just a corner. The Corner has since grown to five city blocks of around-the-clock commercial activity.

U.Va. was founded in 1819. Thomas Jefferson, then retired from his two terms as president of the U.S., was the guiding force behind the movement to establish a state university in central Virginia. The site for the school was about a mile west of the rural town of Charlottesville, in a rocky field at the crest of a hill on a farm once owned by James Monroe.

A community grew up around U.Va., comprising a village separate and distinct from Charlottesville—known throughout the 1800s as "University, Virginia." It was not until 1916 that Charlottesville annexed the little village of "University." This tour will guide you through the historic "downtown" district of the village of University, Virginia—known for the past one hundred years as "the Corner."

Park in the Fourteenth Street garage. Take the elevator down to the ground floor and turn to left as you exit. Head up the stairs and head east on Wertland Street.

1 **1301 Wertland Street, Wertland (c.1829)** William Wertenbaker built this home between 1828 and 1830, and called it "Wertland." Wertenbaker was appointed by Thomas Jefferson as librarian of the University in April of 1826, and served in that post until his retirement in 1881. Wertland Street is today lined with elegant, turn of the 20th-century homes, most of which have been converted into student apartments. Famed artist Georgia O'Keefe spent her summers on Wertland Street while teaching drawing

classes at the U.Va. summer school from 1912 to 1916. The reputed address of her family's home is 1212 Wertland Street.

Walk down Wertland Street and turn right on 12th street, then walk down to W. Main Street.

2 **1211—1215 W. Main Street (1826, mid-1800s)** A handsome Federal townhouse was built in 1826 on land purchased from Jefferson's master builder, James Dinsmore, and construction is attributed to him. It has Flemish bond brick work, a mousetooth cornice, stepped gables with an attic thermal window and delicate fanlight and side lights at the entrance. The small entrance portico and two-story enclosed side porch are 20th-century additions. From 1838 to 1913 the house was occupied by the family of Clement P. McKennie (1798—1856), who co-founded Charlottesville's first newspaper in 1820. McKennie was also the founder and proprietor of the University Bookstore which opened at the Corner in 1825. The building to the west, the "Annex," was probably built in the mid-1800s and may have been used as student housing.

3 **1223 W. Main Street, University Baptist Church (1928—1929)** This large impressive structure has its origins in the High Street Baptist Church built in 1901. In the 1920s the congregation decided to relocate here, closer to the University, in order to provide a house of worship for students. The six-columned brick church was designed by Richmond-based architect Herbert Levi Cain.

4 **George Rogers Clark Monument, (1919)** On the south side of the street is a statue of frontiersman, George Rogers Clark. Designed by Robert Aiken and unveiled in 1919, the site is framed by hemlocks, sycamores and pine trees. The statue was a gift to the city by Paul G. McIntire, native son and prolific benefactor.

5 **The C&O Railroad Bridge** The Chesapeake & Ohio railroad tracks were laid through the University community around 1850, and were originally level with the road at this point. By the late 1890s there were nearly thirty passenger trains running through the neighbor-

hood each day, as well as an increasing number of pedestrians, horses and wagons, and bicycles, so the grade crossing on University Avenue had become rather precarious. A cut was dug in 1901 and the street was lowered to accommodate the bridge and its tracks. Students of the University used to paint the results of successful athletic events on this bridge, giving it the familiar name "Bridge of Scores."

6 1405—1409 University Avenue, Chancellor Annex (1930) This one-story brick annex to the Chancellor Building replaced a series of wood-framed shops that had been on the site since the mid 1800s. African-American brothers Charlie and William Brown operated their popular barbershop on this site for decades. The White Spot, a Corner institution since 1953 is the best known business in the annex today.

7 1411—1415 University Avenue, The Chancellor Building (1914) Built on the site of the original University Bookstore, the Chancellor Building is named for pharmacist Samuel Chancellor, who operated Chancellor's Drugstore in the storefront farthest to the west. Part of a major renovation of the Corner in the years before World War I, the Chancellor Building offered one-room apartments for students upstairs and three storefronts below. When the structure was first built, U.Va.'s boxing coach Johnny LaRowe operated his famous billiard parlor out of the middle storefront.

8 1412 University Avenue, The Corner Building (1914) The University's Corner Building was designed by Eugene Bradbury. It was originally referred to as the "Entrance Building" since it was located at the entrance to the school's grounds. With a string of storefronts, the Corner Building has the distinction of being the first "strip mall" in Central Virginia. When first built, it housed a post office, book store, clothing store, and a fancy tea room.

9 Senff Gateway (1915) Mrs. Charles Senff donated money for the new gateway in honor of her deceased husband and in commemoration of the University's honor code. Architect Henry Bacon, who designed the Lincoln Memorial in the nation's capital, crafted the look of the dual gateway—using Harvard University's 1901 gates as a model. Unlike the crude turnstile that had once marked the entrance to the grounds here, the new Senff Gateway was designed to accommodate both pedestrians and automobiles.

10 1416 University Avenue, University Medical School (1927—1929) There has been a School of Medicine at U.Va. since the institution's opening in 1825. The most famous graduate is Walter Reed, the "conqueror of yellow fever," who received his diploma in 1869 at the age of 17. The Medical building—known as the Ennion G. Preventorium—was completed in 1929 at the cost of $1,400,000. Additions were made in 1936.

11 1415 University Avenue, Anderson Brothers Bookstore Building (1891) Richard Dabney Anderson and his brother John bought George Massey's bookstore on this site in 1876. The current building, the Corner's flagship high-rise, was erected in 1891. With two floors of student apartments upstairs and room for a large bookstore and sporting goods business downstairs, Anderson Brothers was one of the longest running businesses in the Corner's history, closing in 1988.

12 1427 University Avenue, The Sheppe Building (1925) Pharmacist William H. Sheppe's University Drug Store occupied this building when it was first erected in 1925. Notice Sheppe's name towards the top of the structure, and the name of the business set in tile at the doorway. Sheppe's soda fountain was a big hit with generations of University students.

13 **1501 University Avenue (1925)** This building was home to the University Grocery Store in 1925. Just off the alleyway to the right was Carlton Van Lear's infamous pool hall, which closed in 1971. To the west in the 1920s was a tree-shaded lot which contained the Kitch Inn diner which opened in 1922 and was famous for its all-night waffle specials.

14 **1515 University Avenue (1927)** With two storefronts and student apartments, this building was added to the front of a private home. The home, which is still visible if you walk down the side of the building to the parking lot in back, was built in the mid-1890s and was owned by the Minor family. The exit from the Corner Parking Lot, known as Minor Court, follows the route of the home's driveway. The ground floor originally consisted of two storefronts. The Cavalier, a popular gathering spot for students until World War II, occupied the left side. Eventually the entire first floor was occupied by Lloyd's Rexall Drugstore from 1957—1993.

15 **1517 University Avenue (1920)** Both students and faculty at the University initially objected to its construction, having been opposed to a commercial operation this close to the Rotunda. There were originally two storefronts in this building as well. One of the first businesses in this location was Mrs. Ellie Page's Open Door Tea Room. A number of women in the University community entered the business world by opening tea rooms and boarding houses in the early 20th century. The University Cafeteria, nicknamed the "Uni-Caf" filled this space from 1942—1983.

16 **1521 University Avenue, The Virginian Restaurant (1923)** A U.Va. tradition, The Virginian is one of the oldest restaurants in Charlottesville, having been in operation since the fall of 1923. The walls of the eatery are lined with photographs from The Virginian's history.

17 1527 University Avenue (1923) Like many other buildings at the Corner, this building had two storefronts when it was built, one of which was an A&P grocery store. Mincer's Pipe Shop (originally located elsewhere on the Corner) opened in the left store front in 1954. The right space, which had previously been a shoe store and men's clothing store, was home to Red Rohmann's Sporting Goods Store from 1960-1985.

18 Elliewood Avenue Perhaps Charlottesville's liveliest dead-end street, this avenue was named around 1910 for Ellie Wood Page Keith (1894-1986) whose mother ran a boarding house for many years on the site now occupied by Eljo's Clothing Store. Once a quiet, residential lane of boarding and rooming houses, most built in the years before World War I, Elliewood Avenue became a bustling thoroughfare of restaurants, bars, and shops in the 1970s.

19 1601 University Avenue (1927) Stevens-Shepherd Clothing Store occupied this site from 1942 until 1965, followed by Ed Michtom's clothing shop from 1965 until 1976. both stores kept male University students outfitted in the traditional coats and ties that were once so much a part of U.Va. life.

20 Chancellor Street Named for James Edgar Chancellor, a physician at the University who helped care for sick and wounded soldiers here during the Civil War, the early 20th-century homes on this street were renovated during the 1970s and many of them converted into sorority houses. Female students were first admitted to the University as nursing students in 1901. In 1920 women were permitted to enroll in graduate progams. The College of Arts and Sciences did not admit its first official co-educational undergraduate class until 1970.

21 1700 University Avenue, St. Paul's Memorial Church (1927) An Episcopal church was created at the University of Virginia in the early 20th century because the "Episcopal boys" at U.Va. were deemed to be "neglected persons" by the Reverend Robert Gibson, then Bishop of Virginia. A wood-framed

chapel was built on this site in 1910. The present church, designed by architect Eugene Bradbury, replaced it in 1927.

22 **Brooks Hall (1876)** Built as a natural history museum and financed by New York industrialist Lewis Henry Brooks, the University's Brooks Hall of Natural Science opened in 1877. The museum was stocked with an impressive array of natural curiosities—the most talked about of which was a gigantic replica of a prehistoric mastodon, tusks and all. The ornate Gothic building, something of an anomaly at the University, was inscribed with the names of eminent natural historians and adorned with exotic animal heads. The building now houses the Department of Anthropology and the Kevin Barry Perdue Archive of Traditional Culture (Folklore Archive).

23 **1709 University Avenue, Miss Betty's Boardinghouses** Two of the University of Virginia community's well-known boarding houses were located here and were home to generations of students. In 1902 Miss Betty Cocke, a granddaughter of Thomas Jefferson's friend General John Hartwell Cocke, opened a boardinghouse with her sister in a grand home that has since been torn down. Only the front steps remain. Miss Cocke, who lived to be 100 years old, passed away in 1973. Next door, in a house that is still standing and used by U.Va. today as office space, Miss Betty Booker, an opera singer during her younger years, operated a boardinghouse with her mother beginning after World War I. She passed away in 1967.

24 **Madison Lane Fraternity Houses (ca 1900—1910)** The first fraternities at the University were founded in the years before the Civil War. Though they met secretly and enjoyed catered meals together, sharing a common house did not become a tradition until around 1900. During these years, fraternities built palatial homes for their members on Madison Lane and Rugby Road, overlooking U.Va.'s athletic field, now nicknamed "Mad Bowl."

25 **Madison Hall (1905)** Built for the student-run YMCA, Madison Hall opened its doors in 1905 across from the Rotunda. Madison Hall served as a student union building until Newcomb Hall was opened in the fall of 1955. Since 1984 Madison Hall has been the home of administrative offices and today houses the office of the University President.

26 **The University Chapel (1885—1890)** In keeping with his wishes that the faculty not include any members of the clergy or that the school not sponsor any official religion, Thomas Jefferson did not include a chapel in his plans for the University of Virginia. He did agree to set aside a room in the Rotunda for Sunday services, however. Beginning after the Civil War, a movement, led by women, to build a chapel at the University received much support. The cornerstone of the University Chapel was laid on March 30, 1885. The Gothic Revival chapel was adorned with stained glass and opened for use in 1890.

27 **The University of Virginia Rotunda (1826)** Among architects, considered one of the 10 most beautiful structures in the United States, the Rotunda, centerpiece of Mr. Jefferson's "academical village," was completed shortly after his death in 1826. That same year the building hosted a dinner for the visiting Marquis de Lafayette.

Follow the steps around to the opposite side of the Rotunda and enter the building on the ground floor, where tours of the Academical Village begin.

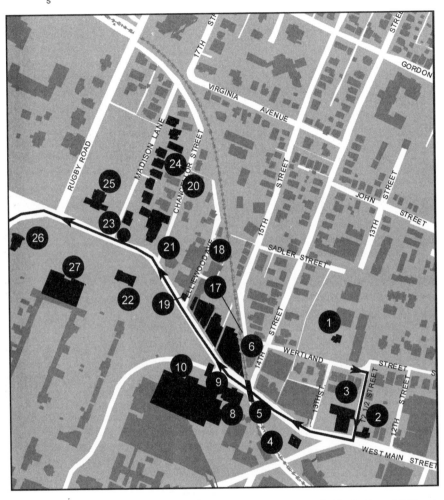

Tour G

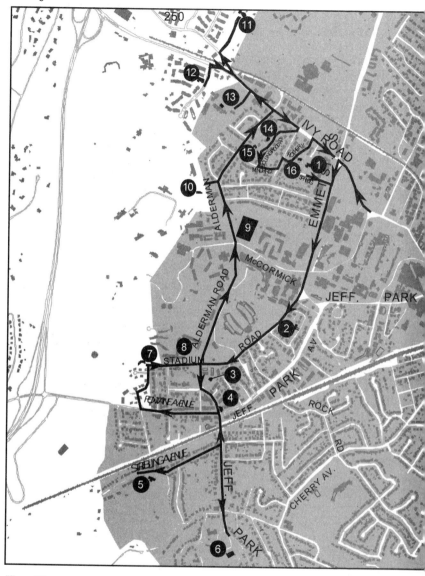

Tour H

1	209—211 Sprigg Lane	6	Fry's Spring Club House	11	2201 Old Ivy Rd.
2	1700 Stadium Rd.	7	121 Mimosa Dr.	12	Lewis Family Graveyard
3	124 Maury Ave.	8	Piedmont Slave Graveyard	13	St. Anne's School
4	2115 Jefferson Park Ave.	9	University and Confederate Cemeteries	14	123 Bollingwood Rd.
5	214 Stribling Ave.l	10	200 Midmont Lane	15	135 Bollingwood Rd.
				16	120 Rothery Rd.

Tour H

SOUTHWESTERN SUBURBS AND PLANTATIONS

This 7.75-mile driving tour consists of several 18th- and early 19th-century plantations that have been incorporated by the city, as well as suburban development around U.Va. The tour begins at U.Va.'s Rotunda, the starting point for Tour I, as well as for the tour of the University given by the University Guide Service (see "For Further Information").

From the Rotunda, drive west on University Avenue. At the traffic light at the foot of the hill, turn left (south) onto Emmet Street, then take the first right onto Sprigg Lane. The first stop is the last house on the right.

1 **209—211 Sprigg Lane, Morea (1835—1842)** John Patten Emmet (1796—1842), who was appointed by Thomas Jefferson as U.Va.'s first professor of natural history, moved out of his pavilion on The Lawn to obtain more space for his menagerie and botanical garden. The name "Morea" is derived from the Latin name for the mulberry trees needed for the silkworm industry that he hoped to establish here. Local builder John M. Perry (c.1776—c.1835; see Tour H, site 2) sold the 106 acres to Emmet in 1834. Construction of the house took place in several stages. The Federal section of two and a half stories is the more sophisticated, with its Tuscan columns and Chinese Chippendale balustrade. There is no indication that the area below the second-story veranda was ever an open porch. Later additions were made by the Duke family, who owned Morea from 1847 until 1895.

Return to Emmet Street and turn right. Pass U.Va.'s 1922—1924 Memorial Gym on the left. After going under a masonry overpass, bear slightly to the right, onto Stadium Road, when Emmet Street swings left. Stadium Road follows the 18th-century Wheeler's Road. Just before the road veers to the left, into Montebello Circle, you will see a brick wall and the entrance to the Montebello House.

2 **1700 Stadium Road, Montebello (c.1819—1820)** Montebello was built by John M. Perry, one of Jefferson's builders, after he sold his home on Monroe Hill and 44 acres of his 643-acre plantation for

the University's central Grounds. Montebello's parapet gables, mould-
ed brick cornice, and flat-roofed Tuscan portico are typical of the
Federal style. Perry's daughter married George W. Spooner, Jr. (1798—
1865), who had worked with Perry on the University buildings. The
Spooners occupied Montebello until 1870.

*Continue southwest on Stadium Road, past U.Va.'s Scott Stadium, to the
4-way stop sign. Maury Avenue is to the left and Alderman Road to the
right. Turn left onto Maury Avenue. It swings slightly to the left after a cou-
ple of blocks.*

3 **124 Maury Avenue, The Anchorage (1913)** This large, stuccoed house with its hipped roof covered by red tile was
designed by architect Eugene Bradbury (see Tour I, site 13) in
the Craftsman style.

*At the traffic light at the intersection with Jefferson Park Avenue and
Fontaine Avenue, look at the service station on your left. (You will pass
it again later.)*

4 **2115 Jefferson Park Avenue (1932)** This unique
Colonial Revival service station has a red tiled roof,
parapet gables, and Tuscan columns.

*Continue straight at the traffic light. (This is also Jefferson Park
Avenue, as it makes a turn at the light.) Cross over the railroad
bridge and take the first right, onto Stribling Avenue.*

5 **214 Stribling Avenue, White Cross/Huntley Hall (1890)**
Stribling Avenue swerves around this large fieldstone house. It
was designed and built by Stephen Price Maury (1850—1941),
grandson of Reuben Maury of "Piedmont" (see Tour H, site 7) and a
partner in the Jefferson Park Land and Improvement Co. (see Tour
H, site 6). The house has some elements of the Shingle style, notably
the horizontal lines, Queen Anne massing, circular tower, and stone
and shingled walls. The acclaimed Charlottesville School for Boys
occupied White Cross in the 1930s.

Return to Jefferson Park Avenue and turn right (south). Keep straight,

between stone gateposts, into the Fry's Spring Beach Club parking lot at the end of the street.

6 **2512 Jefferson Park Avenue, Fry's Spring Club House (1890—1928)** The rambling, half-timbered, stuccoed building you see evolved over three decades from a small weather-boarded club house built in 1890. Summer resorts at mineral springs were very popular in the late 1800s. The Jefferson Park Land and Improvement Co. was organized in 1890 to develop this area and to operate streetcar lines out from the city. The tracks ran along the present grassed median. The first motion pictures in Charlottesville were shown outdoors at the club house in 1905. A large and picturesque summer hotel burned in 1910. There was also a short-lived amusement park. A large swimming pool was built in the 1920s, and the club house was enlarged and remodeled to meet the entertainment needs of a new generation.

Retrace your route along Jefferson Park Avenue to the traffic light. Look across the street at the Colonial Revival service station again. Turn left (west) onto Fontaine Avenue. Go five blocks and turn right at U.Va.'s "Piedmont" sign (two blocks beyond Piedmont Avenue). The road leads to the rear of the house, before turning to the right.

7 **121 Mimosa Drive, Piedmont (1806)** The house faces north, toward an abandoned section of Wheeler's Road. The oldest part was built by Reuben Maury (1785—1869), first cousin of oceanographer Matthew Fontaine Maury and grandson of Dr. Thomas Walker (see Tour A, opening paragraph). It has grown to its present form through many additions over two centuries. The small dependency east of the house is an ice house with an office above. The Piedmont estate once included 2,300 acres. General George Armstrong Custer had his headquarters here during part of the four-day occupation of Charlottesville in March 1865. William Jennings Bryan was entertained at a luncheon on Piedmont's lawn in 1897.

Turn right at the house and follow Mimosa Drive to Stadium Road, and turn right. Stadium Road follows the route of Wheeler's Road. At the 4-way stop sign at the intersection of Stadium Road with Alderman Road and Maury Avenue, pause and look to your left.

8 **N.W. corner of Stadium and Alderman Roads, Piedmont Slave Graveyard** The graveyard for the enslaved community at Piedmont is located in the courtyard between two U.Va. Dormitories. There is not a good place to park and no markers to see. The graves in most 19th-century country cemeteries were marked with fieldstones, which were lost over time. U.Va. altered its building plans for this site after being alerted to the presence of the graveyard by a Maury descendant. The Maury family graveyard was located two blocks south of the house, across Fontaine Avenue. Those graves have been moved.

Turn left onto Alderman Road and pass on the other side of Scott Stadium. Go through the traffic light at McCormick Road, and immediately turn right onto Cemetery Road. Parking is by permit, but there is room to pull off and get out for a few minutes to see the cemeteries. Located side by side, the Confederate Cemetery has a statue in the center and is surrounded by a brick wall, and the University Cemetery has a stone wall.

9 **Alderman and Cemetery Road, University and Confederate Cemeteries** The University Cemetery was established in 1828 and is still in use. Many professors and their families are buried here, including two members of the original faculty, Charles Bonnycastle (1792—1840), Professor of Natural Philosophy and Mathematics, and George Tucker (1775—1861), Professor of Moral Philosophy.

During the Civil War, over 21,000 wounded were cared for in temporary hospitals set up in buildings throughout Charlottesville and the University. Buried here in the Confederate Cemetery are 1,097 of those who died. Few of the graves have markers, but there is a plat showing the location of each grave, and all of the names are engraved on the monument in the center of the cemetery.

The two stones across the driveway from the two cemeteries mark the graves of University mascots Beta (d. 1939) and Seal (d. 1953). These two remarkable dogs created their own positions in the University community, which no other has been able to fill.

Return to Alderman Road, and continue north. Turn left onto Midmont Lane just past St. Thomas Aquinas Church. The house is on the left.

10 **200 Midmont Lane, Midmont (1760s, 1833—1870)** Part of the lefthand section of this brick house is believed to have been built in the 1760s by the Lewis family. British officers imprisoned at "The Barracks" five miles northwest of Charlottesville during the American Revolution were allowed to rent the house, and they are believed to have created the terraced garden behind

it. The righthand section of the house was built during its ownership by the Maury family, 1833-1870. Thomas Walker Maury (1779—1842), brother of Reuben Maury of "Piedmont"(see Tour H, site 7), conducted a school in the house in the late 1830s. The house was sacked by Union troops in 1865. Later additions are by the Chamberlain family, who bought the house in 1903.

Return to Alderman Road and continue north to the traffic light at Ivy Road (Rt. 250). Turn left (west). At the next light, bear right onto Old Ivy Road, go through an underpass, and turn right at U.Va.'s "Miller Center" sign. Old Ivy Road follows the route of the Three Notch'd Road (see Tours B and E).

11 **2201 Old Ivy Road, Faulkner House (1850s, 1907)** The central portion of the main block of this house is believed to have been built in the 1850s by Addison Maupin (b. 1813), who purchased the property from the Lewis family. The original front is on the other side of the house. Washington architect Waddy B. Wood designed this Colonial Revival portico and the side wings of the main block in 1907 for U. S. Senator Thomas Martin (1847-1919). The house was later used as a country inn, and was acquired by U.Va.in 1963 and re-named in honor of William Faulkner, who had been writer-in-residence at U.Va., but had never lived in this house.

Return to the traffic light, and turn right onto Ivy Road (Rt. 250). Turn left onto Colonnade Drive at the "U-Heights" apartment sign. Turn right at the second driveway. You will be able to see the stone-walled graveyard ahead on the right.

12 **Colonnade Drive, Lewis Family Graveyard** This is the graveyard of the Jesse Pitman Lewis (1763—1849) family. Their house stood on the site of the Faulkner House (see Tour H, site 11). Two Revolutionary War soldiers are buried here. Lewis's daughter

Elizabeth (1791—1867) married Reuben Maury of "Piedmont" (see Tour H, site 7).

Return to Ivy Road and turn right, back toward town. Keep straight at the first traffic light, then turn right at the entrance to St. Anne's-Belfield School. Follow the left fork of the driveway up the hill to the white administration building.

13 **2132 Ivy Road, St. Anne's School (1927)** Founded by the Episcopal Diocese of Virginia in 1910 as a girls' school, St. Anne's moved to this site in 1939. It merged with Belfield School in 1975 and is now coeducational. At the top of the hill is an elaborately detailed, white, stuccoed building with tiled roof, ornate chimneys, and arched windows and doors with twisted columns. Now used  as the Administration Building, it was designed by architect Eugene Bradbury and built in 1927 for Elizabeth Bisland Wetmore (1861—1929), who had achieved fame as a young journalist in 1882 when her newspaper, *The New York Herald*, sponsored her in a race around the world against Nellie Bly, of *The New York World*. She finished in 74 days, two days after Nellie Bly, but six days ahead of Jules Verne's *Around the World in Eighty Days*.

Return to Ivy Road and turn right (east). Keep straight at the Alderman Road traffic light, and take the next right, onto Cameron Lane; then immediately bear right onto Bollingwood Road.

14 **123 Bollingwood Road, Keithwood (1884)** This large, weatherboarded farmhouse pre-dates the suburban development of the area. It faces north,  toward the old Three Notch'd Road. Ellie Wood Page Keith (see Tour G, site 18) operated a very popular riding stable here from the 1920s into the 1980s and taught riding to several generations of Charlottesville children.

15 **135 Bollingwood Road (1935)** This early example of the International Style, rare in Charlottesville, features a curved brick wall and

bands of casement windows. It was designed by Philadelphia architect Kenneth Day.

Turn left onto Minor Road, left onto Cameron Lane, and right onto Rothery Road.

16 **120 Rothery Road, Recoleta (1939—1940)** The planning and construction of this Spanish Colonial Revival house, with its tiled roof and grilled windows, was described by Agnes Rothery (Mrs. Harry Rogers Pratt; 1888—1954) in her 1944 recollections of life in Charlottesville in *A Fitting Habitation.*

Turn right onto Ivy Road and return to the tour's starting point at the Rotunda.

Tour I

RUGBY ROAD THROUGH GRADY AVENUE

This drive north along Rugby Road takes the visitor through a residential neighborhood which was originally known as Preston Heights. It was developed in the 1890s when streetcars allowed people to move further from town. Rugby Road has always had U.Va. connections since its earliest times. Its conversion to a fraternity district began in the 1920s and accelerated in the 1960s. Streets that intersect Rugby provide homes and apartments for faculty and students. In the 1920s the University's School of Architecture came to prominence. The works of many of its graduates are found in this area as well as throughout the city. Please note that traffic is terrific in all University areas, parking is at a premium. You are advised to drive slowly and with care. The tour covers 1.7 miles and takes about an hour.

1 **1910 Carr's Hill Road, Carr's Hill (1912—1913)** On a small hill where Rugby Road runs into University Avenue is Carr's Hill Road and at the top is Carr's Hill, home to the University's presidents. This Colonial Revival building of Flemish bond with a two-story Doric portico was designed by the firm of McKim, Mead and White. On this rise, in the late afternoon of March 2, 1865, General George Armstrong Custer met with the mayor of Charlottesville, other prominent citizens and a delegation from the University who persuaded Custer to spare both the University and the buildings in the city.

Immediately on the left as you drive north is:

2 **109 Rugby Road, Fayerweather Hall (1893)** This rectangular building was the University's first separate gymnasium. Designed by the Norfolk firm of Carpenter and Peebles, it had one of the longest in-door tracks in the country. It is said to have had the University's first bathtubs in the dressing rooms. It now houses the University's Department of Art.

3 **155 Rugby Road (1934)** This brick and marble neo-Palladian building houses the University's Fine Art Collections and is open to the public. It was designed by Baltimore architect, Robert E. Lee Taylor (1882—1953) who worked on the restoration of Colonial Williamsburg and by Edmund S. Campbell (1884—1950) the University's Architecture School chairman from 1927—1950.

4 **Madison Bowl** The large depression to your right, known as "Mad Bowl," is a 3-acre playing field and a gathering place for students. Madison Lane (see Tour G) which runs along the opposite rim of the bowl contains fraternity houses dating from 1900—1928 which are brick variations on the Classical Revival style.

Look across the bowl to the far end of the Lane.

The house with the parapet gable on the facade is St. Anthony Hall home to the Delta Psi fraternity (1900) which is the oldest extant fraternity house.

5 **161, 163, 167 Rugby Road (1911—1922)** These three fraternities, next to the Bayly Museum grouped around a courtyard, are more examples of the numerous Georgian Revival buildings in the area.

6 **169 Rugby Road, Zeta Psi House (1926)** Even a casual glance shows that this structure was based on Monticello with its octagonal end wings and single-story Doric portico. It was designed in 1926 by Louis Voorhees (1892—c.1975) of the University's architecture faculty, who was probably influenced by Fiske Kimball (1888—1955) founder of the University's Department of Architecture who had a role in the restoration of Monticello.

7 **Beta Bridge (1855, c.1920s)** Named after the Beta Theta Pi fraternity which stood on the south-east end, the bridge crosses the C&O railroad tracks and was originally built of wood. It was rebuilt in cast-concrete in the 1920s to withstand the weight of auto-

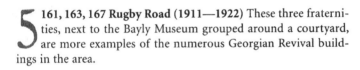

mobiles. Initially concrete lamp posts adorned either end of the bridge but students used them for pistol practice and the city had them removed. Now there are five-foot obelisks topped with metal urns. In the 1890s, the south side of the bridge was a streetcar terminus for the Charlottesville and University Railway Co. complete with turntable.

8 **190 Rugby Road, Westminster Presbyterian Church (1939)** Architect Marshall Wells (1900—1974) member of the University's first architecture class adapted the Abingdon Parish Church of Gloucester County for this building's design. The church's 1980 organ is a Taylor and Boody Opus 3 which is a hand-crafted, tracker-action instrument built in the 17th-century German Style.

9 **203 Rugby Road, Faculty Apartments (c.1920)** This is a Georgian Revival building designed by Fiske Kimball in 1917 as an athletic facility. It was converted into apartments by Professor Edmund S. Campbell. Its classical portico and scaled down upper story are reminiscent of Jefferson's style.

Continue up Rugby Road to the traffic light. You are passing through a bloc of fraternity and sorority houses many of which were originally built as private residences. At the junction of Grady Avenue and Rugby Road, turn left onto University Circle.

Developed from 1908—1925 this area contains 54 houses and apartments. Its residents during that time were a who's who of University people.

Drive carefully as this street is narrow and house numbers are capricious at best and nonsensical at worst. The second house on the right is:

10 **2 University Circle (1910—1915)** This home was originally built for Professor John H. Neff (1887—1938) a popular Medical School professor. Now apartments, it is an interesting combination of the Colonial Revival and the Eclectic styles. *Two doors down is:*

11 **3 University Circle (c.1910)** This Queen Anne style home was built for William Hotopp (1863—1925), founder of the Monticello Wine Co. (see Tour C). It is a frame dwelling of two and a half stories with a steep hip roof and a porte cochere.

Across the street on the left is:

12 **14 University Circle (1908—1910)** This is an interesting combination of Georgian and Mediterranean styles. The house has a red tile roof and stucco walls.

Further along on your left is:

13 **1824 University Circle, Hillel House (1913—1914)** A mansion in the English Vernacular style, it was built of masonry with a smooth white stucco finish. It has a Doric columned loggia on the ground floor and exposed terra-cotta flues. It is one of the city's most sophisticated houses. The B'nai B'rith Hillel Foundation purchased the house in 1945 and it serves as a Jewish student community center. This is one of several houses on the Circle designed by noted architect Eugene Bradbury (1874—1960) who established his Charlottesville practice in 1907. His work can be seen in over fifty area homes and buildings.

In the curve of the Circle, on your right is:

14 **21 University Circle (1914)** This is a good example of Georgian Revival architecture with a front entry porch featuring Doric columns and pilasters. It is another Bradbury design. Originally built for the Macon family it now houses the University's International House.

Across the street is:

15 **20 University Circle (1915)** Here, Bradbury created a splendid example of domestic architecture of the Eclectic style.

Further around the Circle, on your right, is:

16 **35 University Circle (1960)** Designed by Milton Grigg, noted for his work on Monticello, this features a portico over an arcade which Grigg first used in restoring Jefferson's Edgemont in the 1930s. The house belonged to John E. Manahan who married Anna Anderson, the supposed Anastasia, daughter of Czar Nicholas II of Russia.

At the T-intersection with University Way, turn right. At the end of the first bloc, on your left and facing south is:

17 **1811 Lambeth Lane (1915)** This is a large house with a two-story Roman Doric porch and pediment roof similar to Monticello. It may have been built by William Lambeth (1867—1944) the University's Superintendent of Buildings and Grounds who was an authority on Jefferson's architecture. The Theta Delta Chi fraternity purchased it shortly after its construction and remains there.

To your right is:

18 **Lambeth Field Colonnade (1911—1913)** Here are the remnants of the earliest University stadium, designed by R. E. Lee Taylor and Edmund S. Campbell. The semicircular ring of poured concrete bleachers has a Doric colonnade. Most of the stadium field has been filled with dormitories.

Overlooking the area to your right the highest peak is Lewis Mountain. The mansion at the top was designed by Eugene Bradbury and built in 1909 for John Watts Kearney. It is often mistaken for Monticello for tourists are told that Jefferson could look down from his mountain top to watch the building of his university. In the distance are the famed Blue Ridge Mountains of Virginia.

Continue on the one way street around the back of the Faculty Apartments and make a left turn on Rugby Road. Proceed again to the traffic light and turn right on Grady Avenue. Turn left on Preston Place, the first street on your left and between two squat stone columns marked "Preston Place" on the left and "Preston Court Apartments" on the right.

All but two of this neighborhood's buildings date from the 1920s. Many of the homes remain single family dwellings. The architectural style is primarily Georgian Revival.

As you turn into Preston Place, the large building on your right is:

19 **1600 Grady Avenue, Preston Court Apartments (1923—1928)** This was built in the Classical Revival style by Stanislaw Makielski (1893—1969). This three-story building has a "U" shaped plan with a rear court and two-story porticos on the west, south and east facades with French doors opening onto each balcony.

Immediately behind the apartments

20 **605 Preston Place, Wyndhurst (1857; National Register)** This white frame farmhouse built in the Vernacular style in the shape of a large "I." It has two stories with a low hip roof, a raised brick basement and a one-story front porch. It was the main building on a large farm which was raided by Union troops during the occupation of Charlottesville. From 1930—1970, Mrs. Charity Pitts ran a student boarding house which was famous for its table. It is now apartments.

Continue around the circle, you will find on your right:

21 **611 Preston Place, Wyndhurst Overseer's House (c.1812—1820)** This small cottage is of frame construction with board and batten siding, with one and a half stories and gabled roof. It has been heavily altered over the years.

Across the street is:

22 **608 Preston Place, Sigma Chi House (1920s)** This home was built for the fraternity in the Georgian Revival style and also uses elements of the English Vernacular Revival.

At the end of Preston Place, turn left on Grady Avenue and continue to the stop light at Grady and 14th Street. Turn right and then take the next right onto Gordon Avenue.

This area was developed in the 1890s by the Charlottesville Land Co. as a part of Preston Heights. This company played a large role in the real estate development of Charlottesville and Albemarle County. Investors hoped for planned industrialization as well as the orderly growth of homes throughout the city. They were, for the most part, unsuccessful in bringing new businesses and factories to the city. But their efforts did lead to expansion in Charlottesville's first suburbs.

Larger homes on Gordon Avenue were two-story frame buildings built in the Victorian Vernacular style. In the 1920s smaller homes came to be the norm but in the late 1970s they were turned into apartments. Buildings at the top of the hill in the 1600 and 1700 blocks of Gordon Avenue are examples of how student housing has come to dominate the neighborhood.

23 **1501, 1503, 1525, 1535 Gordon Avenue (1920s)** These four small brick houses are examples of homes of the period which originally had deep-set porches with columns.

On the left side occupying the whole block

24 **1500 Gordon Avenue, Gordon Avenue Library (1965—1966)** This is the first branch of Jefferson-Madison Regional Library System. Russell Bailey (1905—c.1985), a Charlottesville architect who specialized in library buildings, designed the building to blend with the neighborhood. The arcaded front portico is based on mid-18th-century Virginia buildings.

The next street to your left is known now as Ackley Lane, it is in fact 16th Street. At the end of Ackley Lane is:

25 1600 Gordon Avenue, Martha Jefferson House (1920—1921) This large brick Georgian Revival style home was designed by Leonidas Pope Wheat of Washington, D.C., brother of the owner. Note the monumental wooden entry topped with a swan's neck pediment. Originally known as "Ackley," it is now a retirement home.

26 1602 Gordon Avenue (1894; National Register) This is one example of the larger homes which first graced this area. It was home for several years to U.Va. Professor of History Richard Heath Dabney (1860—1947) as well as to Dabney's son and noted Virginia historian and journalist, Virginius Dabney (1901—1995). The house is in the Eclectic Victorian style with Eastlake-style ornamentation noticeable in the gables and the sunburst roof brackets.

27 1618 Gordon Avenue, First Church of Christ, Scientist (1958—1959) New York architect Raymond Julian (1902—c.1975), who also designed the Charlottesville Presbyterian Church in 1954, derived this brick design from the classic English churches of the 18th century.

In the next block is:

28 1702 Gordon Avenue (1891, 1910) This is the other home from the neighborhood's early development. The home was remodeled in 1910 when its frame construction was given a white stucco exterior. It houses the Phi Sigma Kappa Fraternity.

Return to Rugby Road and continue with Tour J if you wish.

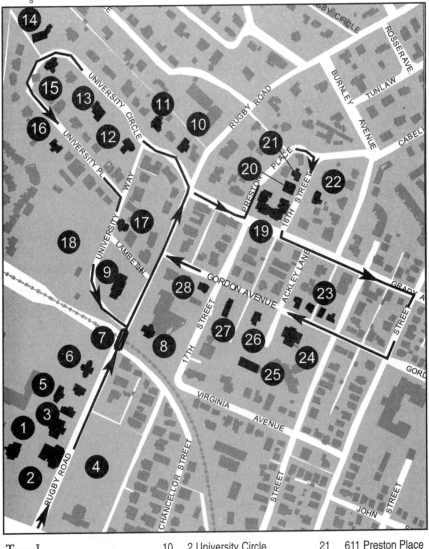

Tour I

1   1910 Carr's Hill Rd.

2   109 Rugby Rd.

3   155 Rugby Rd.,

4   Madison Bowl

5   161, 163, 167 Rugby Rd.

6   169 Rugby Rd.

7   Beta Bridge

8   Westminster Presbyterian
     Church

9   203 Rugby Rd.

10   2 University Circle

11   3 University Circle

12   14 University Circle

13   1824 University Circle

14   21 University Circle

15   20 University Circle

16   35 University Circle

17   1811 Lambeth Lane

18   Lambeth Field Colonnade

19   1600 Grady Ave.

20   605 Preston Ave.

21   611 Preston Place

22   608 Preston Place

23   1501, 1503, 1525,
      1535 Gordon Ave.

24   1500 Gordon Ave.

25   1600 Gordon Ave.

26   1602 Gordon Ave.

27   1618 Gordon Ave.

28   1702 Gordon Ave.

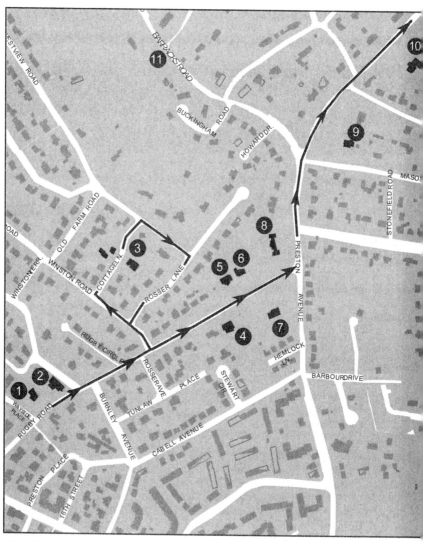

Tour J

1 703 Rugby Rd.

2 Thomas Jefferson Memorial Church

3 908 Cottage Lane, and 907, 909 Cottage Lane

4 928 Rugby Rd.

5 929 Rugby Rd.

6 933 Rugby Rd.

7 936 Rugby Rd.

8 1007 Rugby Rd.

9 1204 Rugby Rd.

10 1314 Rugby Rd.

11 Barracks Rd.

Tour J

RUGBY ROAD NORTH

This tour begins at the junction of Grady Avenue, University Circle and Rugby Road. It takes you though a section of town which included large 19th-century estates which were all subdivided in the 1920s and 1930s creating the neighborhoods we see today. The 600 block of Rugby Road has a few apartments and further down the road is one church. The rest of the road is residential. The tour covers 1.2 miles and takes about half an hour.

1 **703 Rugby Road, Edgewood (1889)** Until the subdivisions, this was the only home between the University and the neighboring estate of Rugby. In 1907, Richard Heath Dabney (see Tour I) purchased the property from his wife's family. His good friend, from their University of Virginia college days, Woodrow Wilson, visited the Dabney family when Wilson was governor of New Jersey.

2 **717 Rugby Road, Thomas Jefferson Memorial Church Unitarian Universalist (1950)** The Jefferson Unitarian Society, organized in 1943, had met previously at the Monticello Hotel in Court Square, Temple Beth Israel and the University Chapel. Designed by Sanislaw Makielski, it is a rectangular brick structure with a high pitched gabled roof and a semi-recessed circular portico.

Turn left off of Rugby in the 900 block onto Winston Road and proceed to the second right turn onto Cottage Lane.

3 **907-909 Cottage Lane, Rugby (c.1850, 1880)** This is the only view you will have of Rugby or Rugby Hall as it was completely surrounded by houses after 1967. Originally on 114 acres, Andrew Brown built a brick home in the Federal style which he used as a school for boys named after the one in England. It was remodeled in the 1880s into a Shingle Style with half-round slate shingles by the then owners Elizabeth Winston Rosser and her husband Confederate General Thomas Lafayette Rosser (see Tour E). In this area General Rosser was famed for his role in the Battle of Trevilian Station in Louisa County, in 1864.

Directly across the street is:

• **907, 909 Cottage Lane (1880s)** These Shingle style cottages were a part of the Rugby estate. Mrs. Rosser ran Rugby as a boarding house and these buildings contained additional rooms for her guests.

Return to Rugby Road by turning right on Westview Road and Rosser Lane which takes you back to Winston. Turning left on Rugby, you will find large stately homes on large lots. On your right is:

4 **928 Rugby Road (1922)** This brick home belonged to Robert H. Webb (1882—1952) who was professor of Greek at the University. The house was designed by Eugene Bradbury in the Colonial Revival style.

On your left is:

5 **929 Rugby Road (1929)** This substantial brick home was designed by Stanislaw Makielski who based the design on Westover Plantation. It may have been Makielski's first residential building. Smaller than Westover, the details appear much heavier than on the home of William Byrd II on the James River. Instead of Westover's flanking wings, there are one-story side piazzas with open decks on top.

6 **933 Rugby Road (1932)** This home was designed by Marshall Wells for the then-president of U.Va., Edwin A. Alderman. The Alderman house is a two-story brick Georgian Revival and one of Wells' first residential buildings. Alderman died before the house was completed but his widow lived there for a number of years.

Last on your right is:

7 **936 Rugby Road, Shadow Brae (1911—14)** Another Eugene Bradbury designed home is this large two-story house with stuccoed walls. It is on a 2.75-acre lot which is one of the larger pieces of property on this stretch of Rugby Road. The family of Dr. Robert F.

Compton (d.1924,) a University Medical School professor occupied the house for fifty years.

Turn west (left) at the traffic light onto a continuation of Rugby Road. Immediately on your left is:

8 **1007 Rugby Road, Belvoir (1928)** A Georgian Revival home designed by Stanhope Johnson (1882—1973,) a Lynchburg architect noted for his Georgian Revival buildings who five years later designed Oak Forest in Farmington as well as the Martha Jefferson Hospital and the Monticello Hotel now 500 Court Square. Belvoir's central pavilion is based on Gunston Hall, George Mason's 1755 home in Fairfax County, Virginia. Wrought iron entry gates lead to the 2.64 acres of gardens and grounds originally designed by noted landscape architect Charles Gillette (1886—1969).

Proceed west and keep on Rugby Road. Do not bear to the left when the road forks and becomes Barracks Road (see number Tour J, site 11). Set back from the road on your right is:

9 **1204 Rugby Road, Stonefield (1860, c.1880; National Register)** The original part of this home, a simple vernacular one-over-one two-story frame structure, is now the southeast or rear portion of the existing house. After 1880, Mason Gordon (1840—1914), local attorney and a member of the University governing body, the Board of Visitors, added a two-story Victorian Queen Anne addition which was two rooms wide and one room deep on the side of the older home. From 1915—1955 this was the site of Stonefield School run by Miss Nancy Gordon (1876—1954).

In the next block on your right is:

10 **1314 Rugby Road, Four Acres (1910; National Register)** This red brick Colonial Revival is another Eugene Bradbury home. It has a tall main block with a large classical portico featuring Ionic columns. It was to be the summer residence of Lucy Cocke Elliott (1875—1969) and Milton C. Elliott (1879—1928), a Washington attorney and Woodrow Wilson's general counsel to the

Federal Reserve. It may be the last house in the city to have hand-hewn interior beams, hand-forged nails and hand-made bricks. U.Va. owned Four Acres in the late 1940s at which time it was occupied by Admiral William F. "Bull" Halsey (1882—1959) who had commanded the Navy's aircraft in the Pacific during World War II.

By continuing out Rugby Road to Dairy Road you will eventually reach the 250 Bypass.

While you are in the neighborhood

11 Barracks Rd. This road is named after the barracks built during the Revolutionary War. It housed Hessian mercenaries and British soldiers captured at the battle of Saratoga. The site is five miles west and no structures are present today.

• **1615 Keith Valley Road (c.1750s—1790s, 1937)** This home began as a log house with large stone chimneys at each end. Architect Marshall Wells persuaded its owners in the 1930s to preserve the old building and incorporate it into a modern dwelling. He added a third smaller chimney to complement the addition.

• **1535 Rugby Road, Trail's End (1914)** This is a large English Tudor building which was built as the Charlottesville Country Club and designed by Eugene Bradbury. Its walls are fieldstone with stucco and half-timbering. It has been the Chi Psi Fraternity house since 1949.

• **Barracks Road, Sunnyside (c.1800, c.1859)** The northern (right hand) section of this rambling frame house was built c.1800. It was enlarged and remodeled in the Gothic Revival style (c.1859), using Washington Irving's home "Sunnyside" in Tarrytown, N.Y., as a model. The house was the home of the Duke family from 1863—1963. There have been many additions and alterations.

Glossary of Architectural Terms

• **American Bond** - See Brick Bond.

• **Architrave** - In classical architecture the bottom portion of the entablature resting on the columns. Also the molding around a rectangular opening (as in Architrave Trim).

• **Balustrade** - A row of balusters (or vertical architectural members having a vaselike outline) topped by a rail.

• **Bargeboard** - A board, often ornamented, that conceals the roof timbers projecting over the gables.

• **Batten** - A thin, narrow strip of lumber used to seal or cover a joint on a board and batten wall.

• **Brick Bond** - The arrangement of the headers, or ends, of bricks that bind a brick, masonry wall. American Bond comprises rows of headers every fourth, or more, courses, while English Bond is arranged with alternating courses of headers and stretchers (or bricks laid out lengthwise). Flemish Bond is composed of alternating headers and stretchers--within each course--arranged to form a plus sign in three courses.

• **Casement Window** - A window constructed with the sash hinged on one side.

• **Chimney Curtain** - A brick parapet wall connecting two gable-end chimneys, and masking the gable roof.

• **Console** - An architectural member projecting from a wall to form a bracket.

• **Corbeled Cornice** - See Cornice.

• **Corinthian Order** - See Greek Orders.

• **Cornice** - Exterior trim at the joining of the roof and the wall, or the top molding on an interior wall. A Dentil Cornice, also known as a

Modillion Cornice, is made up of bricks projecting under a roof eave. A Corbeled Cornice features a series of brick projections, each stepped progressively farther forward with height, used to support and overhanging roof. A Mousetooth Cornice comprises one or two rows of diagonally set brick under a roof eave.

• **Dentil Cornice** - See Cornice.

• **Doric Order** - See Greek Orders.

• **English Bond** - See Brick Bond.

• **Entablature** - In classical architecture the horizontal building member that rests atop the columns, consisting of the cornice (on the top), the frieze (in the middle) and the architrave (on the bottom).

• **Facade** - The front of a structure.

• **Fanlight** - A semicircular window, with radiating ribs like a fan, placed above a door or window.

• **Federal Revival** - A style popular during Jefferson's lifetime—from about 1780 to 1830—featuring fanlights and figural or non-orthogonal spaces, arches, and domes.

• **Flemish Bond** - See Brick Bond.

• **Frieze** - The portion of the entablature (the horizontal building member, in classical architectural, that rests atop the columns) that lies between the architrave (the entablature's lowest division) and the cornice (the entablature's topmost division).

• **Gable** - The vertical triangular end of a building from its eaves to its ridge. A Parapet Gable is one featuring a low wall, sometimes stepped, which receives the gable roof, often serving as a fire wall in townhouses.

- **Gazebo** - A freestanding, open-sided and roofed structure, often on a veranda.

- **Georgian Style** - From the English reigns of three King Georges (1714—1820), an architectural style emphasizing classical correctness and symmetry, featuring brick construction with courses and cornices of white stone and trimmings of painted white woodwork. In Virginia, also includes wood frame buildings too and orthagonal plans.

- **Gothic Revival** - An 18th- and 19th-century architectural style inspired by the Gothic style. Some of the features include slender vertical piers, counterbalancing buttresses, vaulted ceilings, and pointed arches. In Virginia, it occurs from about 1830 until after the Civil War.

- **Greek Orders** - The Composite Order is an elaboration of the Corinthian Order (see next) having acanthus leaves of its capital combined with the large volutes of the Ionic Order. The Corinthian Order is characterized by capitals featuring an elaborate cornice, volutes (or spiral, scroll-shaped ornaments) and two rows of acanthus leaves. (Acanthus was a prickly herb found in the Mediterranean region.) The pure Doric Order column is squat, fluted, and has no base. The pure Ionic Order capital features volutes that lie parallel to the building wall surface. The Tuscan Order is a simplified version of the Doric Order, using a plain frieze (see definition).

- **Greek Revival** - A first half of the 19th century style marked by the use of the Greek architectural orders. In Virginia, from 1830 to about 1860 and features flat transoms and pilasters.

- **Half-Timbered** - Built of wood framing with spaces filled in with masonry.

- **Hip Roof** - See Roof Types.

- **Ionic Order** - See Greek Orders.

- **Italianate** - A style that is basically Italian in its characteristics. Features brackets, coupled rounded windows, and square towers.

- **Jack Arch** - A flat lintel with gauged bricks.

- **Keystone** - The central, wedge-shaped unit of an arch.

- **Lintel** - A horizontal architectural member running across the top of an opening such as a door or window.

- **Loggia** - A roofed-over gallery, usually with open arcades.

- **Louver** - An opening fixed with slanted, and sometimes movable, fins to allow for the passage of air.

- **Mansard Roof** - See Roof Types.

- **Modillion Cornice** - See Cornice.

- **Motif** - A dominant, usually recurring, central theme or thematic element.

- **Mousetooth Cornice** - See Cornice.

- **Palladian** - A revived, classical architectural style based on the works of Italian Renaissance architect Andrea Palladio (1508—1580). Palladian style was imported into England in the 17th century and America in the latter half of the 18th century. Thomas Jefferson referred to Palladio's *The Four Books of Architecture*, reprinted in 1713, as his Bible.

- **Parapet Gable** - See Gable.

- **Pavilion** - A part of a building projecting from the rest, or one of several detached or semidetached units into which a structure is divided.

- **Pediment** - The triangular gable end of a roof located above its cornice.

- **Pendant** - A hanging ornament—sometimes a

pineapple or acorn—used in roofs or ceilings.

• **Piazza** - A large porch, usually with more than four columns and two stories in height.

• **Pilaster** - A wall-mounted flat, rectangular pillar that has both a capital and a base.

• **Porte Cochere** - A passageway through a building designed to allow vehicles to pass through, or to pass from the street to an interior courtyard.

• **Portico** - A covered entry area supported by columns.

• **Portico-in-antis** - A recessed portico in which the columns are flush with the building's outside wall.

• **Queen Anne** - Having the characteristics of early 18th-century English construction featuring modified, classic ornamentation and the use of red brickwork in which relief ornaments are carved. In Virginia, usually after the Civil War in the Victorian Period between 1860 to about 1900 and features circular towers.

• **Quoins** - A pattern of raised bricks, or stones, used to highlight the corners of buildings.

• **Romanesque** - A style of architecture developed in Italy between the Roman and the Gothic styles featuring profuse ornamentation, the use of the round arch and vault, and the decorative use of arcades (or arched, covered passageways). In Virginia, during the late 19th century, often patterned after the architecture of H.H. Richardson.

• **Roof Types** - A Hip Roof is one that slopes upward from all four sides, while a Mansard Roof has a double slope on two sides, the lower slope being much steeper.

• **Rusticate** - To face a structure with rough-surfaced masonry blocks having beveled edges producing pronounced joints.

• **Second Empire** - A style prevalent during the 1852—1870 reign of French Emperor Napoleon III. It features heavy, ornate modification of the earlier, Empire styles. Made popular in America by Alfred B. Mullett and featuring mansard roofs and cresting.

• **Sidelight** - Glass along the side of a door.

• **Spandrel** - The sometimes ornamented area between the exterior curve of an arch and an enclosing right angle.

• **Stucco** - An exterior wall covering usually made of cement, sand, and a small amount of lime.

• **Transom** - A flat window placed over a doorway.

• **Trellis** - A frame of latticework (composed of lattice, or crossed wood or metal strips) used as a screen or for the purpose of supporting climbing plants.

• **Tripartite** - Divided into, or composed of, three parts or sections.

• **Tuscan Order** - See Greek Orders.

• **Veranda** - A covered open gallery or porch attached to the outside of a home.

• **Vernacular** - A non-high style mode of building based upon traditional, regional, or indigenous folk culture.

• **Victorian** - Relating to the arts, architecture, or taste prevalent during the reign of Queen Victoria of England, 1837—1901.

• **Weatherboard** - A sawn board used for horizontal exterior wood siding.

Bibliography

Barefoot, Coy. *The Corner*. Charlottesville, Va., 2001.

Dabney, Virginius. *Mr. Jefferson's University: A History*. Charlottesville, Va., 1981.

DeAlba, Susan. *Country Roads: Albemarle County, Virginia*. Natural Bridge Station, Va., 1993.

Department of Community Development. *Historic Preservation Plan: Charlottesville, Virginia*. Charlottesville, Va., 1993.

Eddins, Joe. *Around the Corner After World War II*. Charlottesville, Va., 1977.

Heblich, Fred T., and Mary Ann Elwood. *Charlottesville and the University of Virginia: A Pictorial History*. Norfolk, Va., 1982.

Heblich, Fred T., and Cecile Clover Walters. *Holsinger's Charlottesville, 1890—1925*. Charlottesville, Va., 1976.

Landmarks Commission. *Historic Landmark Study: Charlottesville, Virginia*. Charlottesville, Va., 1976.

Lay, Edward K. *The Architecture of Jefferson Country*. Charlottesville, Va., 2000.

Loth, Calder, ed. *The Virginia Landmarks Register*. 4th ed. Charlottesville, Va., 1999.

Moore, John Hammond. *Albemarle: Jefferson's County, 1727—1976*. Charlottesville, Va., 1976.

Rawlings, Mary. *The Albemarle of Other Days*. Charlottesville, Va., 1925.

_____. *Ante-Bellum Albemarle*. Charlottesville, Va., 1974.

_____. *Early Charlottesville: Recollections of James Alexander, 1828—1874*. Charlottesville, Va., 1942.

_____. *Historical Guide to Old Charlottesville*. Charlottesville, Va., 1958.

Woods, Edgar. *Albemarle County in Virginia*. Harrisonburg, Va., 1972 reprint.

Work Projects Administration. *Jefferson's Albemarle: A Guide to Albemarle County and the City of Charlottesville, Virginia*. Charlottesville, Va., 1941.